"Dr. Sunita Osborn came on my podcast, WITH WHIT, and I was blown away. Her kindness and knowledge helped me feel so at ease with the mixture of emotions I felt after my first miscarriage. She helped me normalize my complex guilt, and I will be forever grateful. *The Miscarriage Map Workbook* is a must for women who are feeling lost with how to navigate life and emotions after a miscarriage."

— **Whitney Port**, TV & Podcast Personality

"Pregnancy loss can be so isolating and lonely. As someone who has lost many pregnancies, I always found myself searching for hope & healing. Dr. Sunita Osborn's book, *The Miscarriage Map Workbook*, is an amazing tool for all women who've suffered from this excruciating loss. She gets into the real and raw realities of suffering a miscarriage, how it impacts your relationships, and guides you through healing. Nothing can ever take the pain away but knowing there are resources to help women navigate through the pain is revolutionary. This is what women have needed for years."

— **Jamie Otis Hehner**, TV & Podcast Personality, Miscarriage Awareness Advocate

"*In The Miscarriage Map Workbook*, Dr. Sunita Osborn skillfully clears a pathway for families lost in the darkness of miscarriage to begin the healing journey. Her approach leads readers through the process of reflection, reaching out, and resuming life after loss and also models for clinicians how to provide supportive and sensitive care for clients experiencing this specific type loss. For therapists specifically, the "notes to therapists" vignettes give insightful perspective and concrete directives that will surely enrich the work of the therapist and provide deeper healing for clients."

— **Hilary Waller, LPC**, Program Director, The Postpartum Stress Center,
Coauthor of, *Dropping the Baby and Other Scary Thoughts*

— **Karen Kleiman**, Founder, The Postpartum Stress Center,
Author of *The Art of Holding in Therapy*, and several other
books on perinatal mood and anxiety disorders

"As clinicians working with moms focusing on postpartum mental health, we see firsthand the trauma that occurs with moms that have gone through a miscarriage. Dr. Osborn addresses the trauma of a miscarriage through practical, relatable, and empowering interventions. This is a must-have on the bookshelves of health care professionals working with women."

— **Caitlin Slavens, BAACS, MC**, R. Psych.

— **Chelsea Bodie, BSc., MACP**, R. Psych., @MamaPsychologists

"As a miscarriage survivor and advocate, I see such a gap in care between provider and patient in providing resources and options for women going through loss and the time thereafter—physically, mentally, and emotionally. SO many women suffer unnecessarily and anything that can help bridge that gap is a win for women grieving everywhere. As humanity moves forward, I love seeing the medical community make shifts to better care for these women."

— **Kierra Butcher**, Miscarriage Awareness Advocate, @kierra_b_art

"*The Miscarriage Map Workbook* is a fabulous tool for professionals as well as for anyone who has suffered and been impacted by pregnancy loss. Sunita has expertly crafted an easy-to-follow journey toward healing after a miscarriage that will hugely benefit those who utilize it. Her authenticity and experience—both personal and professional—are evident throughout the workbook, offering relatable and supportive texts and exercises. I highly recommend *The Miscarriage Map Workbook* and will most certainly be using it in my therapy practice."

— **Christina Furnival**, Licensed Mental Health Therapist (LPCC),
Author & Blogger at ThisIsRealLifeMama.com

THE
MISCARRIAGE
MAP
WORKBOOK

An Honest Guide to Navigating Pregnancy Loss,
Working Through the Pain, and Moving Forward

A Resource for Women, Couples, Therapists,
OBGYNs, Midwives & Other Helping Professionals

SUNITA OSBORN, PsyD

Copyright © 2021 Sunita Osborn

Published by
PESI Publishing & Media
PESI, Inc.
3839 White Ave
Eau Claire, WI 54703

Cover: Amy Rubenzer
Editing: Jenessa Jackson, PhD
Layout: Amy Rubenzer & Bookmasters

ISBN: 9781683733553
Printed in the United States of America

PESI Publishing
pesipublishing.com

About the Author

 **Sunita Osborn, PsyD, MA**, is the author of the celebrated *Miscarriage Map* and a licensed psychologist who practices in Houston, Texas. She specializes in reproductive psychology and works with adults and couples in all phases of their reproductive journey. After finding herself lost and without a map after her own experiences of pregnancy loss, she is committed to helping women cope with the pain of miscarriage, increasing awareness and decreasing stigma toward miscarriage, and promoting open dialogue on the realities of this prevalent and devastating concern.

DEDICATION

This workbook is dedicated to my husband, Michael. To quote one of our favorite musicals: "I look into your eyes, and the sky is the limit!" Your love and unwavering encouragement make me feel like I can do anything and be anything. To be loved by you is the most special gift I could ever receive. Let's keep reaching for the sky together my love.

Table of Contents

INTRODUCTION

Miscarriage: It can devastate an individual, a couple, and a family to their very core. And yet, this painfully common human experience is so rarely talked about. How do we continue functioning? How do we tell our partner what we need? How do we deal with the emotional roller-coaster that is the aftermath of a miscarriage? How do we not erupt at the fifth person who tells us, "You can always have another baby"? It was in response to questions like these that I decided to write *The Miscarriage Map: What to Expect When You Are No Longer Expecting*, based on my personal experiences with multiple miscarriages, as well as my clinical expertise as a psychologist.

Publishing *The Miscarriage Map* led to numerous conversations about pregnancy loss and highlighted the shocking lack of resources for this painfully common experience. While *The Miscarriage Map* offered a more personal narrative of my experiences with miscarriage, I wanted to create a book that offered practical, beneficial, and engaging exercises and information for individuals, couples, and mental health clinicians. Thus, *The Miscarriage Map Workbook: An Honest Guide to Navigating Pregnancy Loss, Working Through the Pain, and Moving Forward* was created.

This book is dedicated to providing individuals, their partners, loved ones, and health providers—including therapists, obstetricians, and midwives—with the map they need to traverse the painful, shocking, and all-encompassing journey that is a miscarriage. *Miscarriage* is defined as the loss of a pregnancy before 20 weeks of gestation. After 20 weeks, the loss of a pregnancy is defined as a *stillbirth*. Although there has been recent debate about use of the word *miscarriage* due to possible stigma in this word (as the stem "mis" is defined as "mistaken" or "wrong"), the terms *miscarriage* and *pregnancy loss* will be used interchangeably in this book in an effort to capture the words that individuals most commonly use to describe their experiences. Additionally, while this book is written for individuals who have experienced miscarriage as opposed to stillbirth—and there are certainly distinct physical and psychological stressors unique to the experience of stillbirth—it is my hope that this book will still offer some guidance and support for individuals who have experienced stillbirth.

When it comes to the prevalence of pregnancy loss, research shows that one in four pregnancies will end in miscarriage. While that number is strikingly high, the amount of resources available for those who have been affected by miscarriage is just as strikingly low. The lack of resources and dialogue around miscarriage can often leave those affected by this universal issue to wonder about the validity of their reaction. For example, people may wonder, "If no one else is talking about this, is there something wrong with me that I am so upset?" or "If no one else is talking about this, maybe it's not such a big deal." I know I certainly had painful thoughts like this enter my mind after my miscarriages. Thus, this book is for anyone out there who is needing support after a miscarriage or who wishes to support others in the healing process.

For therapists and other treatment providers who are working with clients, this book will provide you with numerous unique exercises that you can tailor to the experiences of your client.

Additionally, it will provide psychoeducation regarding the impact of reproductive trauma, the unique losses experienced by miscarriage, and the steps to take toward recovery. You can use the exercises and psychoeducation provided in this book as a source of exploration in session, or you can give it as homework between sessions. You can also use this book in group settings, with each chapter serving as a topic for group discussion. In this case, give group members the exercises to complete in the session, or assign it as homework to be reviewed at the next meeting.

For individuals, couples, or loved ones, I'm sorry that you have a reason for picking up this book, whether it's because of your own miscarriage or because you want to understand the miscarriage of someone close to you. Traumatic or significant life events can cause our views about ourselves, others, and the world to be fundamentally rocked or changed. This book was designed to help you take the time to slow down and reflect on your experience of loss, including how it has affected you individually, in your relationships, and in your views of the world. It will provide information and guidance to help you navigate some of the common hurdles one faces after pregnancy loss. Further, this book will help you define what "moving forward" looks like and support you in this process. Many of the exercises and information provided along this journey will better equip you to manage the anxieties, grief, and everyday difficulties life can give us with increased compassion, insight, and hope.

A unique feature of this book is that it is written by someone who has been on both sides of the therapeutic couch. I am a licensed psychologist trained to help individuals navigate the perils of trauma and grief, and I have become a client myself when I needed help in processing my own trauma and grief after I had two miscarriages. Thus, the content and exercises of this book are based both on research and clinical expertise, as well as from personal experience as I walked through each of these chapters and challenges myself.

Indeed, you will see parts of my story shared throughout this book as I provide examples to help support you as you complete the exercises. So before you begin sharing about yourself, I would like to take the opportunity to share a little about me.

My Story

I still remember the exact moment I decided I was ready to have children. It was the summer of 2018, and my husband and I had just moved from Indianapolis, Indiana to my hometown of Houston, Texas. We had a house in the suburbs, lived close to my family, and both had amazing jobs with great flexibility. My epiphany came in the car, as most of my epiphanies do, as we were driving to Lake Charles, Louisiana for my husband's thirtieth birthday. I remember the sun streaming into the car and reflecting on how full our life felt, and it hit me—I am ready to have a baby!

My husband and I had no other children, and I had never been pregnant before, so this was all completely new, exciting, and terrifying territory for us. We took a couple of months to plan, explore, and discuss all the what-ifs, and we finally decided we were ready. Well, I was ready two months before, but I graciously gave my husband two months to catch up. We were fortunate enough to conceive fairly quickly and found out we were pregnant in the fall of

2018. My husband and I were both ecstatic, and I remember thinking, "This is happening! This is where it all starts!"

We went for our first doctor's visit and were told that I was definitely pregnant, but it looked like I was a little earlier in the pregnancy than they expected. We were asked to come back again for further testing and repeat ultrasounds. This can be a commonly painful and incredibly anxiety-provoking scenario for individuals who have experienced miscarriage. You are told you are pregnant but are also made aware that the pregnancy may not be viable. The concept of an unviable pregnancy is likely something most of us have never considered—or at least never considered ourselves having to face. I remember, perhaps naively, thinking that pregnancy equaled baby. There were no extra variables in that simple formula. I found myself alternating between attempting to reassure myself that everything would be okay to proactively bracing myself for the worst, thinking that doing so would somehow prevent me from feeling the full extent of the pain. Many of us in this situation find ourselves caught in this emotional pendulum.

After multiple doctor's visits and endless days filled with anxiety, dread, and a smattering of hope, we were finally told I was having a miscarriage, a blighted ovum specifically, in which the gestational sac continues to grow, but the embryo does not. I was devastated, confused, angry, and completely shattered. Plans were made for continued testing, as well as necessary procedures. This is another challenging aspect of pregnancy loss: After you hear the news, you are not able to crawl into bed and allow yourself to begin the grieving process. Depending on your circumstances, you will likely be experiencing painful physical symptoms (at the very least) and surgery at the other end of the spectrum.

After our loss, I struggled to fully confront my grief and did what many of us who have experienced miscarriage do: I tried to become pregnant again and quickly. I remember thinking that if I was able to get pregnant again, my first miscarriage could just be a blip on an otherwise entirely joyful journey. This plan to avoid facing my grief worked, and I found out I was pregnant again in the beginning of 2019. As I will discuss in this book, pregnancy after miscarriage can be incredibly anxiety provoking because thoughts of "What if I have another loss?" continuously intrude into your mind. My worst fears unfortunately came true, and I found out I was having my second miscarriage in the spring of 2019.

Throughout my pregnancies and subsequent losses, I experienced gut-wrenching grief as I never have before, as well as all-consuming anxiety that wrecked me both physically and emotionally. The reverberations of my loss and grief were felt in my body, my mind, my relationships, and in the way I saw the world and my future in it. As with most of life's most excruciating circumstances, my experiences also provided me with a deeper insight into myself and my relationships than ever before. I was confronted by qualities and beliefs I never truly recognized, such as resiliency and perseverance, as well as less attractive qualities, such as resentment and a tendency to focus on the injustices of my situation—"Why did this have to happen to me?"

I share this story with you to illustrate that the words, exercises, and guidance I provide throughout this book are informed not only by my experience as a psychologist and my knowledge in reproductive psychology, but also from my deep knowing and living of the same challenges, pain, and journeys we will take together in this book.

How To Use This Book

To make this book easy to follow, the chapters are ordered sequentially and follow the path of loss to recovery, starting with processing your expectations about pregnancy and sharing your miscarriage story, to developing a list of coping skills and traversing the various phases of recovery and challenges after loss. Therefore, I recommend that you complete each chapter in its entirety before moving on to the next chapter. Additionally, if you are completing this book on your own, I recommend that you have a go-to person for support, whether that be a therapist or friend with whom you can discuss any difficult or painful feelings that come up. It is important to note that there is no "correct" or "normal" way to respond after a miscarriage, and certain chapters or issues may have more emotional salience to you than others. As I will repeat often throughout this book: **Whatever you are feeling is okay. Your process is just that: *yours.***

As you read through each chapter, you will find specific information to help you navigate each step of your journey, including exercises to improve your insight and provide you with guidance, as well as questions to help you process your reaction.

- **Chapter 1: Sharing Your Story.** A significant part of healing involves sharing and processing your story of loss. This chapter will introduce the concept of the *reproductive story*, which is the story we tell ourselves about having children that begins developing in childhood and is then interrupted by miscarriage. I will explain the concept of reproductive trauma and its impact on the developing reproductive story as well. Additionally, this chapter will describe the importance and healing effects of writing and sharing your story. Specific exercises throughout the chapter will guide you through the process of sharing your loss and deepening your understanding of your experience, and it will help uncover your unique reproductive story.

- **Chapter 2: Creating Your Survival Guide.** This chapter will explore the broad range of emotions that may surface after a miscarriage, including sadness, anger, and grief. It will also provide psychoeducation regarding the difference between self-care and self-soothing, as well as the concept of healthy compartmentalization. The exercises throughout this chapter will deepen your understanding of the unique challenges following pregnancy loss and will guide you through the process of creating a tailor-made "survival guide" to help you cope and move toward recovery.

- **Chapter 3: Grieving.** This chapter details the unique experience of grief following a miscarriage, including the experience and impact of disenfranchised grief and the ramifications that occur when you are unable to adequately acknowledge or mourn your loss. It also describes the steps involved in grieving the loss of your dreams, hopes, and wishes—and, for some, the loss of the first joyous and successful pregnancy that they will never get to have. The exercises in this chapter will help you process and mourn this loss, as well as identify any myths you have been taught around grief that may impact the grieving process.

- **Chapter 4: Getting the Support You Need.** This chapter details the experience of sharing your story of loss with others. It normalizes the ambivalence that readers may experience in sharing their miscarriage and discusses the stigma around miscarriage that can often impact an individual's decision to disclose. I'll also share the advantages of sharing your story with others and help you come up with specific language and methods you can use to better communicate your needs with others. Finally, I'll give you some tools to identify your own support squad and overcome barriers to receiving support.

- **Chapter 5: Your Relationship After Miscarriage.** This chapter explores how trauma or loss can affect a couple's relationship, and it describes the overall impact of miscarriage on a couple's connection, priorities, and partnership. In particular, I will discuss various factors that can impact the relationship following pregnancy loss, including differences in the grieving process between partners, changes to physical and emotional intimacy after having a miscarriage, and the benefits of couples therapy following a loss. Exercises in this chapter will help you identify ways to increase connection with your partner and provide you with prompts for guided discussions to help you explore and share your feelings following this loss.

- **Chapter 6: Your Relationship with Your Body After Pregnancy Loss.** This chapter outlines the many changes women may experience in how they view or experience their body following a miscarriage. It normalizes feelings of anger, confusion, sadness, and dissatisfaction that may follow this loss. It also provides research-based insights into the mind-body connection and how a woman may feel betrayed and disconnected from her body as a result of pregnancy loss. Exercises in this chapter include guided visualizations to identify and strengthen the mind-body connection, which is often weakened following a miscarriage, as well as compassion exercises to help you identify ways to show acceptance and gratitude for your body.

- **Chapter 7: Shame After Miscarriage.** This chapter explores the impact of shame following a miscarriage, as well as signs that you may be experiencing shame. It explores the role of stigma in the development and perpetuation of shame following pregnancy loss and describes different manifestations of shame based on family experiences, personal experiences with miscarriage, and interpretations of this loss. Exercises in this chapter will help you identify the recurrent shame-based messages you tell yourself (your "shame tracks") and provide you with specific ways to respond to shame in a way that is congruent with your values.

- **Chapter 8: Moving Forward, Not On.** This chapter outlines various ways to find meaning following a miscarriage and highlights the difference between "moving forward" from your loss versus "moving past" it. It also normalizes the different ways to grieve, noting that there is no correct way to cycle through the various stages of grief. In addition, this chapter will help you redefine what it means to find your own rainbow after pregnancy loss and explores the multiple pathways you can take to find this rainbow, whether that involve wanting to try again, waiting, or deciding to not have children. Finally, the chapter provides some prompts to help you create a life that aligns with your hopes and values.

After my experiences with miscarriage, I felt lost and adrift, wishing for some type of map to help me navigate the emotional storm I was in. It is my hope that this book will provide you with that very map so you can walk through the pain and loss of miscarriage and come out on the other side with more compassion, insight, and hope for the future.

1

SHARING YOUR STORY

> "When we deny the story, it owns us. When we own the story, we can write a brave new ending."
>
> —Brené Brown

Our Reproductive Story

Our **reproductive story** is our narrative of parenthood. It encapsulates all our ideas, hopes, expectations, and dreams about having children and becoming parents (Jaffe, Diamond, & Diamond, 2005). After a miscarriage, we not only have to contend with the physical loss of the pregnancy itself, but we also must face the loss of our reproductive story. Oftentimes, we are not even aware that we have a reproductive story until it is disrupted by pregnancy loss. For example, many individuals may make statements such as "I never thought this would happen to me" or "It wasn't supposed to happen this way." If we were to ask these individuals how they imagined it would happen, that would give us clues into their reproductive story.

The significance of recognizing and naming our reproductive stories lies in the essential role it plays in our healing. We naturally grieve after pregnancy loss, but we also experience feelings of anger, confusion, resentment, and sadness that, at times, leave us feeling stuck and unable to move forward. These feelings largely arise due to our reproductive story having gone haywire following miscarriage, and it is through owning this story and its subsequent disruption that we can reach full understanding of our emotional reaction. For instance, consider the woman who felt a tremendous amount of grief after her miscarriage and described feeling "trapped" in her grief. Through careful exploration of her experience and her reproductive story, we learned that it was not her grief keeping her trapped; rather, it was her feelings of sadness and anger that this beautiful reproductive story—which she had dreamed of since childhood—had been fundamentally disrupted. By understanding and owning this pain, she noted a sense of "release and relief" and found herself able to move more freely through her grief.

Our reproductive stories start forming in early childhood and have their roots in our relationship with our parents. We may look forward to replicating the same positive relationships we have with our parents and think, "I can't wait to be the same kind of loving and fun mother as my mom and create the same wonderful memories I had in my childhood." Alternatively, we may hold fears of following the same negative patterns as

1

our parents and imagine having children as an opportunity to create the kind of childhood we always wished for ("When I'm a parent, I'm going to make sure to raise my child in a completely different way than my father did. I will be all the things I wished for myself.")

Our stories about parenthood are also impacted by our family history, cultural background, peer group standards, and the media. For example, a young girl who grew up in a large family as the oldest child likely took some responsibility in taking care of her younger siblings—whether or not she was developmentally ready to take on this caretaking role. This experience would likely inform her expectations about parenthood and impact the development of her reproductive story. For instance, it is possible that this girl's experience of taking care of her siblings led to a desire to replicate this same role in adulthood with her own children. Alternatively, it is entirely possible that this early experience of having to take care of her siblings cultivated a reproductive story around having only one child or a wish to have no children at all. As mentioned previously, we all carry a reproductive story, even if that story is about not having any children and instead serving as a loving aunt to our family's or friends' children.

Additionally, the significance of gender roles, timing, and other aspects of family planning may vary across cultures. For example, the collectivistic nature of South Asian culture emphasizes the value of having multiple children to continue the family line and to ensure that elders in the family are taken care of. Even as these cultural norms are beginning to shift over time, individuals who were brought up by parents who held these norms are likely to have reproductive stories that are impacted by these beliefs (e.g., "I want to have children earlier and plan to have multiple children").

Alternatively, people from individualistic cultures, such as the United States or Germany, may come from families that value autonomy, self-sufficiency, and the prioritization of individual needs over the needs of the many. These cultural values can, in turn, impact the timing of someone's reproductive story (e.g., "I will wait to have children until I have reached a certain level of success in my career"). To add to the intricacy of these cultural norms, individuals may also receive messages from friends and through the vastness of online media that may coincide or conflict with the cultural beliefs they heard growing up. These factors can all serve to inform the development of one's unique reproductive story.

We can see emerging themes around our reproductive stories in children's play as they act out the role of doctor to their sick dolls or stuffed animals, or when they have their toys take on the role of parents taking care of their "babies." These themes usually center on the role of caretaking and safety that parental figures provide. Additionally, when enacting these sorts of play, children often mirror what they have seen in many children's books or movies, in which a family comprises two parental figures with one or more children. As children get older and move into adolescence, these reproductive stories continue as teenagers often begin fantasizing about parenthood and, even if they don't explicitly acknowledge it, often imagine their partners as parents (Jaffe, Diamond, & Diamond, 2005).

Oftentimes, our reproductive stories are grounded in ease and excitement. We imagine that the process of having children will look the same as it does in movies and will be consistent with the images of parenthood we were exposed to in childhood and early adulthood—

images of joy, simplicity, and certainty. We may excitedly ponder questions such as "How many children do I want?" and "How many years apart do I want them to be?" Perhaps we anticipate having children around the same time as our siblings so they can be close in age, or we wonder if we can try to time the pregnancy so the baby is born around the holidays. While the answers to these questions remain unknown, before pregnancy loss, they are often thought of with joyful anticipation.

After pregnancy loss, these questions take on a drastically different tone as we now contemplate, "Will I ever be able to have children?" or "If I do have children, will it be the way I or my partner want?" or "Do we have the financial or emotional bandwidth to pursue other reproductive options?" The contrast of asking ourselves these kinds of questions after daydreaming about the possibilities of holiday births and spacing between multiple children can feel devastating. In asking ourselves these questions, we are confronted with the reality that our reproductive story has not gone the way we planned. Feelings of loss, anxiety, grief, and depression can ensue, along with a loss of self-esteem and a loss in our sense of control. These feelings, as well as the negative effects they have on our most intimate relationships, are all normal after the reproductive story has been disrupted.

What Is Your Reproductive Story?

Healing comes from being able to recognize and share your reproductive story, processing how it was disrupted, and rewriting the new chapters. If you have written the story once, then it holds to reason that you have the power to rewrite it as you choose. Complete the following prompts to identify your reproductive story. An example of my reproductive story is also listed for your reference.

☐ When I thought of my future family, I always envisioned...

☐ When I imagined pregnancy, I thought about...

☐ When I considered being a parent, I imagined...

☐ Growing up, my upbringing taught me that parenthood...

My Reproductive Story

When I thought of my future family, I always envisioned having a big family with at least three kids. I grew up in a big family, and my fondest memories from childhood were of playing around with my siblings. *When I imagined pregnancy, I thought about* how excited I was to grow this little human in me. I knew my partner would be so tender and supportive, and I looked forward to how special that time together would be.

When I considered being a parent, I imagined being a young parent. I wanted to be able to run around with my kids and still be young when they got older and had grandchildren. I even thought that far along—what my grandkids would be like!

Growing up, my upbringing taught me that parenthood was a beautiful and natural part of growing up. It seemed like my parents' lives—their decisions about their careers, where they lived, and what vacations they took—centered around us kids. Parenthood always seemed like the natural next chapter after finding your partner.

Now take some time to write out your reproductive story using these same prompts.

_____

_____

_____

_____

_____

_____

_____

_____

_____

_____

_____

_____

_____

_____

_____

_____

_____

_____

_____

_____

_____

Reproductive Trauma

Trauma is any event that individuals experience or witness that causes them to fear for their physical or psychological safety. Trauma often involves a threat to our physical integrity, meaning that we feel like our sense of being healthy and whole is in danger. Although many people equate trauma with an experience in which there is an actual threat to our safety, trauma can involve any event that overwhelms our physical or emotional capacity to cope. Indeed, **reproductive trauma** is a type of trauma that includes events such as pregnancy loss and infertility, as both events go beyond the range of usual human experience and can have a significant physical and emotional impact on us. It can cause us to feel devastated, alone, broken in body and spirit, and rocked to our very core. Similar to other types of trauma, these events can also threaten our physical integrity because it involves an experience in which our body does not function the way we need or expect it to.

Pregnancy loss fundamentally disrupts our sense of the past and future. For example, after my experiences of miscarriage, my mind struggled to accept the reality of my situation. I often found myself automatically still thinking of the future in terms of our due date. I would consider the dates of an upcoming conference and immediately begin calculating how far along in my pregnancy I would be. Or, when asked about going on a trip with my in-laws the following year, I automatically begin to wonder how old our baby would be at the time and if we would be able to travel by that point. It took a matter of milliseconds before I was brought back to reality, and I often felt foolish that those thoughts had entered my mind in the first place.

Yet, as I often try to do, I encouraged myself to follow the same guidance I would share with my clients and readers: to share my story. After loss, our mind struggles to make sense of how this once beautiful image of the future has been so distorted from what we expected. *Consequently, we need to be able to tell our stories again, and again, and again until we can make some sense of them and integrate them into our narrative.* Although your path to healing from reproductive trauma will vary based on your unique individual and contextual circumstances, many individuals who have experienced pregnancy loss find significant relief in sharing their story with others. That is because in sharing our stories, we are able to make sense of what happened (Devine, 2017).

Once we allow our stories to be told, it allows us to make the intangible, tangible—which allows for grieving and healing. It takes far more energy to keep negative energy in than it does to express these experiences out loud. Consequently, sharing your story can relieve you of the burden of holding these painful emotions and thoughts under the surface. Thus, in moments that you find yourself forgetting the reality of your situation, direct compassion inward and use this as an invitation to share what you are feeling with someone with whom you feel safe. It can be incredibly helpful and healing to share your story with others and to receive their support and empathy.

Sharing Your Story

Consider someone with whom you feel safe, someone you believe would be unconditionally supportive and caring toward you. Maybe you are even experiencing their warmth and acceptance right now as you picture them. If you feel comfortable, share your reproductive story from Exercise 1.1 with this person. If you are seeking treatment, it may also be helpful to share your story with your therapist or in the context of a support group. Notice how it feels to hear this person's response. Were you surprised by what they had to say? Use the space provided to record any notes or thoughts you had from this experience of sharing your story.

_____

_____

_____

_____

Although I encourage you to share your story, it is understandable if you prefer to not share your story with others at this time. In this case, you can read your story aloud to yourself. Then read it aloud again, but this time imagine that the story you are hearing was written by a friend or family member whom you care greatly about. What would you feel if you heard a loved one share this story? What would you want them to know?

_____

_____

_____

_____

_____

Deepen Your Understanding

An integral step in understanding our story is exploring how the trauma has impacted and potentially changed us. According to cognitive processing therapy (CPT), trauma can fundamentally alter our beliefs about our self, others, and the world when it comes to the following five domains: safety, trust, esteem, intimacy, and power and control (Resick & Schnicke, 1992). For example, when it comes to intimacy, reproductive trauma can interfere with our beliefs regarding self-intimacy (i.e., the ability to be alone without feeling empty or lonely and the capacity to self-soothe) and intimacy with others (i.e., the ability to form close, vulnerable connections with others). In order to heal, it is important to explore how the experience of trauma has impacted you with regard to each domain, both in relation to the self and others. The following is an adapted CPT exercise to help you explore how the experience of pregnancy loss has impacted you.

Exploring Your Story

Go through each of the core areas listed here and consider how pregnancy loss has impacted your beliefs about intimacy, self-esteem, power and control, trust, and safety. There are no right or wrong answers here. For some of these areas, your beliefs may not have changed. Or there may be some areas where your beliefs have already been altered due to past life experiences. Just write what feels true to you and your story.

Intimacy: The longing for intimacy with others is one of our most primal needs. After pregnancy loss, our desire to be close or vulnerable with others may change. This is particularly true if we experience invalidating responses from others or feel misunderstood. Additionally, many individuals who experience pregnancy loss often struggle to be around or feel close to those who have children or who are also in the beginning of starting their own families. This is a common struggle when many of our friends are of similar reproductive age, and watching our friends have healthy pregnancies and subsequent children may contribute to a desire to isolate ourselves.

I used to believe...	I currently believe...
Example: I was an open book. I would share everything with everyone and enjoyed updating my friends with what was going on in my life and receiving the support and happiness for my husband and me.	**Example:** I have become a lot more careful with whom I share. I have gotten so many invalidating comments—like "Well, at least it happened early"—that I prefer just to keep to myself, even with my husband sometimes. It can get pretty lonely.

Esteem: When individuals experience a pregnancy loss, it is not uncommon for them to begin to question their self-esteem or their belief in their own worth as a human being. They may experience self-defeating thoughts such as "If I can't have a baby, does that make me less of a woman?" Or they may deem themselves a "failure" because they are unable to have a successful pregnancy, which affects the way they gauge their worth to their partner, to their family, and certainly to themselves.

I used to believe...	I currently believe...
Example: I have always felt really good about myself and my worth. I am proud of my job and how I am as a wife, sister, daughter, and friend.	**Example:** After my miscarriages, I started having thoughts like "If I can't have a baby, does that make me less of a woman?" I've never questioned myself like this before.

Power and Control: Power and control refer to our sense of agency in the world—our belief that we can solve problems and meet challenges. When we feel like we are in control, we have a greater capacity for self-growth and are more likely to experience a sense of accomplishment. Pregnancy loss can be an inherently disempowering experience because it takes away our control and what happens to our bodies. We also continue to experience a loss of control after experiencing a miscarriage because we must follow guidelines that dictate when we can try to conceive again (if we even desire to), and we may have to make other adjustments to our life that we would not choose ourselves.

I used to believe...	I currently believe...
Example: I'm someone who always believed that if I wanted something enough, I could get it and that I had control in making it happen. It was an empowering way to live because I knew that whatever dreams I had, it was in my hands to make it happen.	**Example:** I started to feel really out of control after my miscarriages. I had no control over the miscarriages themselves, the surgeries I needed to have afterward, or all the money we spent. I felt angry and defeated that all this was happening, and I felt like I didn't have a say in determining my future.

Trust: When we trust in ourselves, we believe that we can rely on our own perceptions and judgment, which is essential for developing a healthy self-concept. However, after pregnancy loss, many individuals experience distrust toward their body's ability to function the way they need it to. Additionally, they may get angry at their own "inability" to know what was happening in their body in the days or weeks leading up to the pregnancy loss. Many women often feel angry and confused that they were unable to detect the signs they were having a miscarriage (e.g., "How did I not know what was happening inside of me?").

I used to believe...	I currently believe...
Example: I have definitely been someone who has trusted myself to reach my goals and to do what I needed to do, whether it was something in my career or something I wanted to do physically, ranging from rock climbing to horseback riding.	**Example:** After my miscarriages, I really started to doubt myself. Clearly I couldn't count on myself to reach my own dreams—aka having a healthy pregnancy. I also have a much more jaded view of my body and what it can do now.

Safety: As humans, we have a basic need for safety. We need to believe that we can protect ourselves from harm and that we have some sense of control over the events in our lives. For many of us, this expected sense of safety also extends to our ability to protect our unborn children. Therefore, when pregnancy loss occurs, it can be particularly painful as we question our ability to keep ourselves or our babies safe (e.g., "I should have been able to protect my baby from this" or "If I can't even protect my baby in the womb, how will I ever keep a baby safe?").

I used to believe...	I currently believe...
Example: When I was pregnant, I felt confident that I was doing everything I could to keep my baby safe: taking prenatal vitamins, exercising safely, and also avoiding all the things I usually love, like wine and rock climbing.	**Example:** Now I feel like there's nothing I can do to keep my baby safe. I'm scared to even consider pregnancy again because I can't guarantee safety to my baby or even to myself.

Consider how your current beliefs about each of these five areas have affected you. Have they impacted your relationship with yourself or with others? Take a moment to reflect and respond to the following prompts.

What stood out to me from this exercise was:

_____

_____

_____

_____

_____

_____

_____

_____

What surprised me the most was:

_____

_____

_____

_____

_____

_____

_____

_____

What I want to tell myself after completing this exercise:

_____

_____

_____

_____

_____

_____

_____

_____

_____

_____

Notes for Therapists

If you are a therapist working with a client who has experienced reproductive trauma, the reproductive story is an effective therapeutic tool that can help clients move toward healing. You can use it as way to provide psychoeducation by explaining the significance of this narrative and how it develops, as well as a way to help clients deepen their understanding of their unique internal experience and what their loss means to them.

For some clients, it will be easy to help them identify their reproductive stories. For example, many clients may share that they "have always dreamed of" being a mom or dad. Other clients may have not had such clear ideas about parenthood and will need more support in identifying their reproductive story. Even individuals who do not want to have children have a narrative about parenthood. That is to say, we all carry a reproductive narrative with us, whether or not we are consciously aware of it. To help clients identify their reproductive story, you can ask them questions, such as those listed here. As mentioned previously, children's play often reveals the development of themes and beliefs related to the reproductive story. For example, a child who often played "Mommy" to her toys may have found this a comfortable and desired role versus the child who never took on a parental role to her toys.

- What was your favorite doll or toy growing up?
- What games did you like to play best growing up?
- What does family mean to you?

Additionally, it is helpful to utilize clinical assessment skills to dig deeper into a client's response to these questions. For example, consider this hypothetical response to the question: "What was your favorite doll or toy growing up?"

Client:	Oh that had to be my stuffed doll, Skippy.
Therapist:	Tell me more about Skippy. What would it look like when you were playing with Skippy?
Client:	Skippy was a stuffed baby doll that I used to carry around with me everywhere! There are even photos of my family on vacation with me holding Skippy. Most of the time, I would be feeding her, tucking her to sleep, and arranging playdates with my other dolls.
Therapist:	It sounds like you really enjoyed taking care of Skippy.
Client:	Yes, I've always been that way with my toys growing up and with animals I would come across. In my friend group, I'm even known as the "mom" of the group because I always...[*client continues to describe the "mom" role she has taken in various areas of her life, as well as her enjoyment of this role*]

This client's responses indicate that she has a tendency toward caretaking and enjoys nurturing others. The therapist could use this insight to examine the client's desire to fulfill that role in adulthood, including what that has looked like, as she uncovers her reproductive story.

Additionally, it can be beneficial to examine clients' attachment history—including their history of being cared for and responded to by others, as well as the way they internalize and understand relationships—in eliciting more information about their ideas about parenthood. For example, you can ask:

- Whom did you go to when you were sad or upset as a child? How did they respond?
- Who played with you as a child? What did play look like?
- What did you think about your parents' marriage? Did they seem happy?

All of these questions can give us greater insight into the client and their ideas about themselves and parenthood. Exploring these questions can also shed further light into the ways in which certain clients process their losses. For example, if a client reports that their caregiver parented in an inconsistent manner—sometimes attuning to the client's needs while being emotionally unavailable at other times—then that client may have developed an anxious attachment style as an adult, causing them to experience more anxiety and worry after loss. In contrast, clients who display more avoidant attachment tendencies may have more trouble accessing their emotions. After loss, these clients may experience some sense of psychological distress but will likely struggle to name or understand their reaction. They may also utilize defense mechanisms, such as dissociation, which can disrupt their natural grieving process.

Part of our job is to help clients understand how their trauma impacts them in the context of their conscious or unconscious beliefs about parenthood and adulthood. Parenthood is often seen as a key task in development toward adulthood. Thus, clients may consciously or subconsciously ask, "How can I be an adult if I can't be a parent?" This same identity conflict may occur in the context of gender norms as well. Clients may question their womanhood or manhood based on their ability to have a successful pregnancy.

Ultimately, helping clients to recognize their story, to name it, and to acknowledge how it has been disrupted will serve as the foundation for the rest of your work together. Once clients have written their reproductive story, they can come to learn that they can add new chapters to this story of their choosing. This realization can be very helpful in instilling hope and allowing clients to become active versus passive participants in their healing.

2

CREATING YOUR SURVIVAL GUIDE

> "Being a mom is hard work.
> Becoming a mom is hard work, too."
> —Candace Wohl

Undefining "Normal"

"I shouldn't be this sad."

"I don't understand why I can't just get it together."

"Miscarriage is so common, so it shouldn't be affecting me this much."

Sound familiar? One of the most challenging aspects of life after miscarriage is the set of expectations we hold regarding how we "should" be responding. Because pregnancy loss is so rarely discussed, we have a limited understanding around what is "normal" after it occurs.

No matter where you are at in your journey—whether it's your first miscarriage, your second, third, or so on—please remember there is no "good" or "right" way to respond following this loss. Much of our anxiety, in all scopes of life, is related to the idea that there is a "correct" way of doing things, and we endlessly compare what we are doing, thinking, and saying to this magical, perfect standard. These expectations often extend to the prescribed amount of sadness and grief we believe we are "allowed" to feel. As with most things in life, there is no correct answer here. There is no correct way to cope or an appropriate amount of pain you should feel after pregnancy loss, but there are ways that you can make the immediate aftermath more challenging than it already is—and that includes getting upset at yourself for feeling upset.

Think of it this way: Sadness, grief, and anger are all completely expected responses after loss. However, if we decide that it is unacceptable to experience these painful emotions (or a certain amount of these emotions), then we will attempt to get rid of them by suppressing them. However, when we attempt to suppress a normal response to a challenging situation, another painful emotion usually takes its place—that emotion being guilt. That means that instead of "getting rid" of one negative feeling, all we have done is replaced it with another.

Essentially, we feel bad (guilty) for feeling bad (sad, jealous, or resentful). This dilemma is called a **double bind**, and it often leads to increased and compounded emotional distress (Wojnar, Swanson, & Adolfsson, 2011). That is because guilt serves as a signal that we have somehow done something wrong by feeling sad or angry, and this guilt drives us (whether consciously or unconsciously) to punish ourselves for our supposed wrongdoing. We may punish ourselves by engaging in a barrage of self-critical or self-blaming thoughts, or we may do so by lashing out at others because we do not know how to manage the maelstrom of emotions inside us.

Attempting to qualify how you should react after pregnancy loss simply creates a cascade of other painful emotions and actions. One way to normalize your reaction is to know that there is a host of symptoms and experiences, both emotional and physical, that are very common after pregnancy loss. Consider the following exercise as you reflect on your emotional experience after loss.

Symptom Checklist

There is a wide range of emotions, thoughts, and behaviors that one can expect after a miscarriage. For example, women often feel a whole host of uncomfortable emotions around pregnant women, including sadness, jealousy, and resentment. The frequency, intensity, and duration of these symptoms can vary day by day, sometimes even hour by hour. Again, feeling "all over the place," or as if you are on an emotional roller-coaster, is normal. Use this checklist to indicate which symptoms you have experienced as a result of miscarriage.

_____ **Emotional distress.** Feeling a wide range of distressing emotions, including sadness, grief, anger, shame, anxiety, or depression

_____ **Panic attacks.** Feeling sweaty, sick, disconnected, shaky, and out of control

_____ **Insomnia or problems with sleep.** Finding yourself unable to sleep because you are worrying and thinking a lot about your loss—or about other concerns that keep you awake

_____ **Nightmares.** Having nightmares related to your loss when you are able to sleep

_____ **Feeling tired all the time** even if you have managed to get enough sleep

_____ **Intrusive thoughts.** Being unable to control when images or thoughts related to your loss appear in your mind

_____ **Flashbacks.** Feeling as if you are reliving your loss (as if it is happening right now)

_____ **Difficulty concentrating** or remembering things

_____ **Phobias.** Feeling very scared or anxious about something specific, perhaps related to your loss (but not always)

Take a moment to consider your reaction to this list. Were you surprised by any of the symptoms listed? Have there been symptoms you have experienced that were not listed? Write your reflections below.

_____

_____

_____

Fighting Quicksand

The alternative to attempting to mold our experiences into what we assume is "normal" is allowing ourselves to feel what we are feeling with acceptance and compassion rather than judging or fighting these very normal reactions to loss. We give ourselves permission to fully lean into our experience without attempting to change it, solve it, or get rid of it—which, as we know, is usually impossible anyway. These principles of acceptance and compassion are at the core of an empirically supported intervention known as acceptance and commitment therapy (ACT), which is an action-oriented approach to psychotherapy that stems from traditional behavior therapy and cognitive behavioral therapy. ACT promotes the use of mindfulness and acceptance strategies to cope with the hardships that often coincide with living (Hayes, Strosahl, & Wilson, 2009). Instead of struggling against painful feelings, ACT encourages you to accept these feelings while you continue to take actions that will benefit your life.

According to ACT, the more we try to fight difficult feelings, the more they smother us. It is much like falling into quicksand—the more you struggle, the more you sink. You feel sad, disappointed, or angry, and then you feel sad, disappointed, or angry for having those feelings in the first place. As your difficult emotions grow exponentially larger, your struggle intensifies, and you fall beneath the surface. Instead, what if we allowed ourselves to turn off that struggle switch and let our uncomfortable emotions just *be* there? To just float on the surface without fighting them and without justifying them?

Essentially, when we keep our "struggle switch" on, our emotions remain stuck and we waste a huge amount of energy and time struggling against them. In addition, we often create even more pain for ourselves because we feel disappointed by our disappointment. Alternatively, if we are able to turn our struggle switch off, then our emotions are free to move, we don't waste time or energy fighting against them, and we don't generate any more pain than that which we are already facing.

A simple way to accept uncomfortable feelings is to say, "This too" whenever you notice any painful feelings, thoughts, or sensations come up. Paradoxically, the more that you begin to accept your emotions as they are, the more quickly they seem to pass. As well-known psychotherapist and author Carl Rogers stated, "The curious paradox is that when I accept myself just as I am, then I can change" (1961, p. 17).

Permission Slip

We often struggle against allowing ourselves to feel and experience reactions that are completely normal after pregnancy loss, whether it's certain emotions (e.g., sadness, anger) or certain thoughts (e.g., "Why does she get to have a healthy pregnancy and I don't?"). It can be hard enough to sit with these thoughts without also trying to fight them or reprimanding ourselves for having these thoughts in the first place.

Instead, what if you gave yourself a permission slip to act and feel a certain way? We typically think of a permission slip as a piece of paper that someone in a position of authority gives to someone to allow them to do something. For instance, you can think of a parent signing a permission slip for their child to join an after-school club. But permission slips don't just apply to children. We can also give ourselves a permission slip to accept whatever emotions, thoughts, or sensations we may be experiencing after pregnancy loss (Brown, 2018).

Take a look at the example permission slip provided here, and then create your own permission slip. Your permission slip is unique to you. It may involve giving yourself permission to feel a certain way (e.g., sad, upset, or angry) or to act a certain way (e.g., not forcing yourself to smile or to put on a brave face). It may also involve giving yourself permission to take specific actions, such as declining that baby shower invitation or saying no to that new project at work. These permission slips will allow you to set an intention regarding how you want to show up in different situations.

Here's an example:

I give myself permission to: *not smile if I am not feeling happy. To slow down with my yeses and to allow myself to feel sad when I hear about other people's pregnancies.*

You have permission to say yes,
to say no,
to change your mind,
and to do what is right for you.

Signature: _____   Date: _____

Now try creating your own:

I give myself permission to: _____

_____

You have permission to say yes,
to say no,
to change your mind,
and to do what is right for you.

Signature: _____   Date: _____

I give myself permission to: _____

_____

You have permission to say yes,
to say no,
to change your mind,
and to do what is right for you.

Signature: _____   Date: _____

I give myself permission to: _____

_____

You have permission to say yes,
to say no,
to change your mind,
and to do what is right for you.

Signature: _____   Date: _____

How to Cope: Self-Care versus Self-Soothing

Now that we've acknowledged and given you permission to experience the different reactions you may be having, let's explore how to cope with those reactions by defining **self-care** versus **self-soothing**. The concept of self-care has become heavily commercialized and is often used as a punch line for pleasurable activities. For example, "I'm getting my nails done—self-care!" or "I'm taking myself shopping—self-care!" or even "I'm buying myself this new cell phone—self-care!" To be clear, none of these activities are inherently bad for you and likely will lead to a boost in your mood. However, these activities are not necessarily forms of self-care; they are forms of self-soothing (Schlessinger, 2019). **Self-soothing** activities help us feel better in some way and provide us with a distraction or increased comfort, but they do not lead to long-term healing.

Self-care, on the other hand, is geared toward healing. Self-care is what it sounds like: It is actually taking care of yourself and attending to your physical, emotional, relational, or financial needs. For example, take a situation where I felt stressed after one of my friends asked me to plan her baby shower. For me, self-soothing involved the decision to take a bubble bath while watching my favorite show. Engaging in this activity allowed me to feel a temporary sense of calm as I was able to distract myself from my anxiety and stress. Alternatively, self-care in this situation would involve initiating a conversation with my friend to let her know that I did not feel emotionally ready to plan her baby shower. Again, this is not to state that one method is better than the other. Indeed, we sometimes need to self-soothe before we can feel emotionally stable enough to engage in the work of self-care. For example, in my situation, I needed to engage in a self-soothing activity to help me feel more grounded and less distressed *before* I could have that difficult conversation with my friend.

The following table further clarifies the difference between self-care and self-soothing by providing some examples of each.

Self-Care Activities	Self-Soothing Activities
• Going to therapy	• Taking a bubble bath
• Meditating	• Going on a coffee date with yourself
• Exercising	• Practicing aromatherapy
• Accepting ownership of your finances	• Keeping a gratitude journal
• Saying yes or no when you *really* need to	• Binge watching your favorite show
• Eating the right food for your body even if it isn't what you want	• Coloring
• Eating regular meals even if you only want to snack	• Putting on a face mask
• Going to sleep early when you're tired	• Giving yourself a facial
• Keeping boundaries	• Knitting
• Seeking medical care for physical ailments	• Reading
• Confronting difficult conversations with thoughtfulness and maturity	• Making your favorite meal

As a note, there may be times where you notice that there is overlap between the activities you engage in when it comes to self-care and self-soothing. For example, working out consistently is a form of self-care because it keeps you physically healthy and provides a whole host of long-lasting benefits. At the same time, working out can also serve as a self-soothing activity for some people. For example, after a stressful day, hitting the gym or going for a run may allow some people to decompress and relax. The intent here is not to draw a distinct line between self-care and self-soothing but to ensure that you are making space for both of these activities in your life and getting these needs met.

Build Your Self-Care and Self-Soothing Arsenal

To help build your survival guide, consider what activities currently make up your go-to self-care versus self-soothing routines. If you, like many of us, often struggle to both care for and soothe yourself, consider ways that you can improve or add to your self-care and self-soothing routine. Feel free to use some of the examples listed in the previous table if you need some inspiration.

I currently engage in self-care by:

_____

_____

_____

_____

_____

_____

_____

I will improve my self-care by (e.g., working on clarifying my boundaries or starting therapy this month):

_____

_____

_____

_____

_____

_____

_____

I currently engage in self-soothing by:

_____

_____

_____

_____

_____

_____

I will improve my self-soothing by (e.g., practicing new ways to calm my emotions, such as pottery or gardening):

_____

_____

_____

_____

_____

_____

Healthy Compartmentalization

Pregnancy loss has a way of consuming much of our lives. Physically, our bodies are still reeling and recovering from the pregnancy, loss, or subsequent treatments. Logistically, we often have to attend follow-up appointments and get tests done, which can disrupt our regular schedule and eat up most of our day. Emotionally, we are faced with an onslaught of painful and exhausting emotions. Financially, there are often numerous doctor's or hospital bills we must contend with, and we may be considering assisted reproductive technology that will cause further financial stress. All in all, our lives may feel as if they revolve around pregnancy loss, and we physically or mentally have no escape.

As a result, it can be incredibly beneficial to engage in healthy compartmentalization when it comes to your miscarriage. Compartmentalization is a defense mechanism that we use to isolate and "block off" incompatible values, beliefs, or emotions that cause us to experience emotional distress (Bowins, 2012). When we compartmentalize, we separate any competing segments of our life into different sectors, or compartments. For example, someone who is a ruthless and unforgiving manager at work may use this defense mechanism to separate their "work self" from their "home self" so they can maintain the view of themselves as an honest and family-oriented person.

While defense mechanisms often have a negative connotation, there are instances when using such mechanisms is actually the healthiest response to a stressful situation. For example, we often (subconsciously) utilize defense mechanisms as a protective measure if our mind is not ready to accept a certain reality or needs to diffuse the intensity of our reaction. In the case of pregnancy loss, healthy compartmentalization involves allowing the space for your normal reaction and grief, while also allowing space for other parts of your identity that are outside of pregnancy loss. The journey of trying to become pregnant, becoming pregnant, and then experiencing a miscarriage can create an "identity crisis" in which your entire identity centers around becoming a parent. As a result, other essential facets of your identity—such as your professional identity, your interests, your strengths, or your passions—remain dormant.

To use compartmentalization, consider putting pregnancy loss in its own "psychological container" and isolating it from the other facets of your identity (Jaffe et al., 2005). **By intentionally focusing on aspects of yourself that are outside of the miscarriage, you can come to the realization that you are more than your experience of pregnancy loss.** This can aid you in supporting your strengths and passions, which can ground you during your healing. For example, maybe you have a passion for running and decide to sign up for a marathon. Or perhaps you are passionate about your career and decide to focus on that exciting opportunity that you put on the back burner during your reproductive journey. Or maybe there are some hobbies you enjoy but have not been able to engage in because of pregnancy, such as skydiving or skateboarding.

Further, our identity is not solely defined by what we do or by our roles, but it also includes our strengths and personality traits. Therefore, as you intentionally focus your attention to other facets of your identity, consider your personality traits and internal strengths. Perhaps you have always admired your courage, resilience, vulnerability, or compassion. Allow yourself to bring these traits to the forefront and guide you during this time. After loss, we often have trouble connecting with ourselves and may have thoughts such as "I just don't feel like myself anymore." This is completely normal, and at the same time, it can be helpful to intentionally remind yourself of the parts of you that you previously valued and admired. We are often told that time heals all wounds, and while there is some truth to this adage, I will often encourage clients that it is not just time that heals our wounds but, rather, what we do with this time that leads to healing.

This intentional movement toward focusing on other aspects of your identity can be incredibly helpful in healing your relationship with your partner as well. After pregnancy loss, couples often feel as if their relationship has been consumed by trying to get pregnant, and then experiencing pregnancy loss, and then recovering from that loss. After miscarriage, many non-pregnant partners will state that they have experienced not just the loss of their baby, but also the loss of their pregnant partner as this partner retreats inward. Again, while it is completely normal and helpful to allow yourself time to grieve, it is also essential to tap into your strengths to support your healing. For example, consider the couple whose strength lies in their shared love of community and service. After their experience of loss, they may tap into this strength by directing some of their focus into opportunities to help and support their community, perhaps even around the topic of pregnancy loss. Taking another more personal example, one of the common bonds and passions in my relationship with my husband is our shared love for all things play, whether that is skateboarding, rock climbing, or spontaneous water balloon fights. Intentionally focusing on this part of ourselves felt like a breath of fresh of air after moments of feeling suffocated by grief.

I remember a specific instance when we were returning from yet another doctor's appointment, and we were both feeling so exhausted from the fertility merry-go-round we were on (really the worst imaginable ride). We called upon our shared value of play and decided to stop by a playground on our drive home and just ran around like overgrown children on the slides and swings. It was simple and easy and exactly what we needed to remind ourselves of who were outside of pregnancy loss. While loss may understandably mute these parts of ourselves in our relationships, intentionally reminding ourselves of their presence and importance can provide a significant source of relational support and comfort.

Similar to taking the time to reflect on your own identity, it can be beneficial to consider the many aspects that make your relationship special and unique outside of pregnancy. Consider what you love about your relationship and what strengths you want to draw on to help you and your partner during this time. For example, reflect on the early days of your relationship, and recall what it was that you and your partner connected over and could talk about for hours. Were there certain topics, such as a shared love of superhero movies, or a shared passion around certain activities, such as baking or listening to Broadway musicals? Additionally, the strengths in your relationship extend past the activities and passions you share. It also includes the attributes you hold as a couple, including your ability to be compassionate toward each other in even the most painful of circumstances or to maintain your playful sense of humor even in the face of uncertainty.

Reuniting You with Yourself

Pregnancy and life after pregnancy loss can become all-consuming, leading us to neglect essential parts of our identity. Reunite with the parts of yourself and your relationship that may have been lying dormant by responding to the following prompts.

Before I decided to start my reproductive journey, I was most excited about:

Example: Enjoying our new house was definitely a huge source of light for me. I really enjoyed having fun projects to work on, like building our new deck and getting to know our neighbors. I had also just joined a book club with some friends and was looking forward to getting back into my love of reading.

_____

_____

_____

_____

Before I decided to start my reproductive journey, I would spend my weekends and evenings:

Example: Typically, we would alternate between hanging out with friends and family. We would try out new restaurants and bars and occasionally take road trips. My favorite was when we would spontaneously just book one night at a place a couple of hours away. Those weekends felt like such adventures.

_____

_____

_____

_____

Before I decided to start my reproductive journey, my professional goals were:

Example: Engaging in some new trainings and creating a consult group with other therapists. The trainings were long and comprehensive, but I knew they would be engaging and super helpful to my work.

_____

_____

_____

_____

Before we decided to start our reproductive journey, my favorite way to spend time with my partner was:

Example: Playing tennis, rock climbing, and just spending time together trying out new restaurants and taking road trips. We also love traveling and would have just as much fun planning our next trip as we would taking the vacation itself.

_____

_____

_____

_____

Based on these reflections, what activities, interests, or passions would you like to commit to re-engaging in?

Example: I didn't realize how long it had been since I have seen some of my friends. I want to commit to reaching out to some of my close friends and making a plan to see them. I stopped going to the book club when it began to conflict with the timing of my doctor's appointments. I also want to get with my partner and reinstate our Monday rock climbing dates.

_____

_____

_____

Survival Guide

I encourage you to come back to this chapter whenever you are in need of guidance and support. There will be some days when you just need a healthy distraction from your pain, in which case you will find it helpful to look at your self-soothing list. Alternatively, there may times when you need to remind yourself that you do have an identity outside of experiencing pregnancy loss, in which case you can review your reflections from Exercise 2.4. Last, there may be times when you need to look over the symptom checklist to remind yourself that what you are feeling is completely normal and that it is okay to allow yourself to feel what you are feeling without doing anything at all. And remember, keep that permission slip handy!

NOTES FOR THERAPISTS

As I have discussed throughout this chapter, there is a wide range of symptoms that are considered "normal" after pregnancy loss. However, if you become concerned about the severity of certain symptoms or worry about the safety of one of your clients, it may be necessary to provide them with a higher level of intervention. For example, if clients report difficulties in maintaining a normal level of functioning for a prolonged period of time, this could suggest that additional interventions are necessary. Similarly, if clients report suicidal ideation with intent or a specific plan, it's important to consult with other professionals and to consider more extensive treatment options.

In helping clients develop their survival guide, feel free to be creative and intermix tools and techniques from your theoretical background. While many of these exercises are based in ACT, there are several techniques from the field of cognitive behavioral therapy (CBT) that can be effective in managing a client's distress and that can help them challenge any cognitive distortions or core beliefs that may be showing up. For example, you can provide psychoeducation to clients around the development and impact of cognitive distortions, which are inaccurate or faulty ways of thinking, and highlight cognitive distortions that may be common after pregnancy loss. Many clients exhibit polarized thinking, or the tendency to think in all-or-nothing terms, after pregnancy loss, as evidenced by statements like "I am never going to have a healthy pregnancy" or "I'm always going to feel this sad." Helping clients identify these distortions and challenging them with CBT techniques, such as Socratic dialogue (e.g., "What would you tell a friend who was having these same thoughts and feelings?"), can help clients manage their distress and better equip them to manage future stressors as well.

While you do want to help clients manage their distress, you want to be careful about sending the message that they need to reach for a coping skill anytime they feel distressed. ACT uses the term "experiential avoidance" to describe our attempts to avoid experiencing certain thoughts, feelings, memories, physical sensations, and other internal experiences even when it may cause harm in the long run (Hayes, Wilson, Gifford, Follett, & Strosahl, 1996). Therefore, while there may be moments when clients will benefit from engaging in certain self-soothing techniques to reground them and help them function, you also want to ensure that you are still supporting the natural feelings of pain, grief, and loss that follow miscarriage.

Finally, to help clients reach healthy compartmentalization, make sure to spend enough time exploring your client's sense of identity. When clients begin their reproductive journey, the focus of their identity centers around trying to get pregnant and then trying to heal from pregnancy loss. Due to the sheer number of doctor's appointments and tests that clients may require after pregnancy loss, many individuals can feel like their core identity is that of the "sick patient." It will be important to help clients see that their experience of pregnancy loss is a part of their story but that it does not define their personhood or identity.

3

GRIEVING

> "We always think we're supposed to make grief smaller, but the reality is: We have to become bigger."
>
> —David Kessler

Myths About Grief That Need Debunking

As a society, we are ill-prepared to face loss. We are taught throughout our lives how to acquire things but are given no guidance in how to deal when we lose them. Consequently, there are many faulty, incorrect, and just plain harmful myths out there about how we should deal with pregnancy loss. It's important to identify and debunk these myths because they can often lead to feelings of shame and isolation on top of an already painful experience.

Myth #1: *Don't feel bad.*

Truth: While some people may explicitly tell you not to feel bad following a miscarriage (e.g., "Don't be sad, you can always try again"), others may share this sentiment in more subtle ways. For example, someone might say, "You will feel better soon," which is just another version of "Don't feel bad." While this person may have the best of intentions, this message is dismissive and unrealistic because it invalidates the reality of what you are feeling right now and will continue to feel for the foreseeable future. You will feel bad. You will feel all sorts of bad, including pain, sadness, devastation, and anger—the whole gamut of bad. And that is okay. It is okay not to be okay.

Myth #2: *You can just replace the loss.*

Truth: The notion that you can replace the loss of one child with another is a particularly relevant myth that individuals frequently encounter after a miscarriage. It is not uncommon for others to ask, "Well, when are you going to try again?" or "Why don't you just adopt?" Whether or not you to decide to take any of these steps, there is no replacing what has been lost. It is normal for you to continue to feel and grieve the impact of pregnancy loss.

Myth #3: *Time heals all wounds.*

Truth: Many people adhere to the common adage that time heals all wounds, but it's what you *do* with that time that actually leads to healing. Imagine if you broke your arm. It's not the mere passage of time itself that heals that wound. It's going to the doctor, getting an X-ray, wearing a cast for eight weeks, and living a life that is not normal for a while that leads to healing. Similarly, time alone does not heal the grief from a miscarriage. It's what you do with that time, including intentionally making space for your emotions, thoughts, and experiences through reflection, conversations with supportive others, and healing exercises, such as those included in this book.

Myth #4: *Miscarriage grief is related to how long you have been pregnant.*

Truth: Research has shown no association between the length of pregnancy and the subsequent grief experienced by a woman, yet many individuals invalidate their experience of grief because they believe they have not been pregnant long enough to substantiate their pain. This myth is then reinforced by statements from well-meaning others, such as "It was so early though, right? So you weren't that attached yet." A woman who lost her child at five weeks may be just as devastated as a woman who lost her child at 23 weeks.

Myth #5: *Miscarriage grief is related to how long you have been trying.*

Truth: Similar to the previous myth, individuals may believe the intensity of their reaction must be weighed against the duration of time they have been trying to conceive. For example, consider the woman who says, "I shouldn't be this sad. We only just started trying, while my friend has been trying for years." According to Dr. Janet Jaffe, a physician and co-author of *Unsung Lullabies: Coping with Infertility and Loss*, "No matter how far along you were, when a pregnancy fails, you lose a part of your reproductive story. You have experienced a reproductive trauma" (2005, p. 154). There are no set standards when it comes to how we respond to grief.

As you consider these myths, reflect on which statements feel familiar to you and which ones you have been told. We explore and unpack these myths because they can each impact the way in which we process and reflect on our loss. For example, if I have heard the myth "Miscarriage grief is related to how long you have been pregnant," and I take this as truth, I may then decide I am only allowed a certain level of sadness for my pregnancy that was lost at 10 weeks. Believing this myth can harm my healing because it puts limits on the amount of grief I believe I am entitled to feel. Additionally, it is often because of myths such as these that individuals become "stuck" in their grief. These myths halt the natural progression of the grieving process, which requires emotions to be freely expressed.

Alternatively, there may be other statements you have been told about grief that may be beneficial to intentionally remember and keep with you. What feels helpful to you will be highly individualized and likely unique to your experiences and background. For example, some may have specific ideas about death and loss based on their religious or spiritual background that offer a sense of comfort (e.g., believing that the baby is in Heaven now). Other sentiments about loss—such as "grief can come in waves"—may also serve as normalizing reminders for what you are experiencing.

What Have You Been Told About Grief?*

Review the list here, and check off any statements you have been told or have heard others say about grief and loss. You may find that you relate to all of them or just a few based on your history and environment. This list will help personalize your road to recovery because these beliefs, concepts, and statements impact the way you experience and understand your loss.

As you read through the list, please note that this exercise is not intended to criticize anyone who has told you these statements. Many of us have used these same or similar statements before to comfort others. However, creating this list will allow you to identify which statements are helping or hindering your grief recovery.

_____ Don't feel bad.

_____ Replace the loss.

_____ Time heals all wounds.

_____ At least it happened early.

_____ You can always have another kid.

_____ At least you know you can get pregnant.

_____ Just stay strong.

_____ I know exactly how you feel.

_____ Be thankful you have other children.

_____ This was God's plan.

_____ It was for the best.

_____ All things happen for a reason.

----

* This exercise has been adapted from *The Grief Recovery Handbook* (James & Friedman, 2017).

Write down any other statements you have been told about grief and loss:

_____

_____

_____

_____

_____

After checking off the statements that you have been told about grief, identify the statements that are helping versus hindering your recovery. Put a star next to the statements that you have found helpful, and draw a line across those that have gotten in the way. Consider including the list of helpful statements as part of the survival guide you created in Chapter 2 so you can look at it whenever you need words of support and encouragement.

_____

* This exercise has been adapted from *The Grief Recovery Handbook* (James & Friedman, 2017).

Disenfranchised and Incomplete Grief

The grieving of pregnancy loss is a complicated, painful, and often confusing process. While grieving the loss of your child, you are also mourning the dreams, hopes, and desires you had for your child that was never able to be born. Additionally, while dialogue around pregnancy loss is slowly increasing, there is still a lack of understanding in our culture regarding how to respond to it. That's because the grief following a miscarriage falls into the category of what's referred to as **disenfranchised grief**, which is grief that cannot be openly acknowledged or publicly mourned because it is deemed socially unacceptable to do so (Doka, 1989). Grief becomes disenfranchised when society believes that our relationship to the deceased is "too distant" or somehow "not worthy" of grief. Other losses that fall into this category include the loss of an ex-spouse or infertility.

The problem with disenfranchised grief is that it can cause you to doubt whether you are entitled to your grief. You might ask yourself, "If my community does not count this as a 'real' loss, then how can I?" After pregnancy loss, many of us experience this painful dilemma as those in our inner circle question the validity of our loss through statements such as "There wasn't a baby anyway, right?" or "You can always try again." When individuals make comments such as these, it is likely that they have the best of intentions. They likely want to make you feel better and to make your grief not feel so all-consuming.

At the same time, it is also likely that they want to make themselves feel better. Most of us have had the experience of sitting with someone in pain. We experience discomfort in the face of suffering and often stumble around in our mind trying to figure out the "right" thing to say or do. In turn, we grab at any statement or action that we believe might make things better or make the discomfort feel more tolerable—even temporarily. However, it is statements such as these that can cause us to wonder if we are entitled to grieve. You may wonder, "Were my losses worthy of the sadness, devastation, and pain that I felt?"

As a society, we are ill-prepared to respond to grief and to support those around us who have experienced loss, really any kind of loss. The death of a loved one and the subsequent grief that follows is a universally human experience. And yet, even though we will all experience grief at some point in our lives, there is little formal or even informal recognition of the impact of loss.

Apart from the invalidation and pain caused by disenfranchised grief, there are also dangers in not allowing yourself to fully grieve your loss. This type of **incomplete grief** occurs when there are internal or external factors that prevent you from fully acknowledging and healing from the loss. For example, you may divert your attention to other people's needs as a means of avoiding your own painful feelings and reactions (internal barrier), or you may lack the time or space to fully process your loss due to work or family obligations (external barrier). Signs that suggest you are experiencing incomplete grief include:

- **Uncharacteristic irritability or anger.** Emotions such as sadness, regret, or grief following a loss may manifest as anger or irritability because these emotions often feel safer to express.

- **Hypervigilance and fear of more loss.** After a loss, life can feel more fragile, and you may start to consistently scan your environment, waiting for the next tragedy to strike.

- **Relational changes**. You may cling more tightly to your loved ones for fear of losing them, or you may swing to the other side and distance yourself from others to protect yourself from further pain.
- **Addictive or self-harm behaviors.** In an attempt to distract or numb yourself from pain, you may start engaging in risky or harmful behavior, such as over-drinking, binge-eating, or workaholism.

The alternative to incomplete grief is **grief recovery**, which is the process of being able to fully acknowledge, reflect, and process your loss (James & Friedman, 2017). It means giving yourself permission to feel a full range of emotions, from sadness about what has been lost to joy when reflecting on past fond memories. Grief recovery means waking up one day and realizing that your ability to talk about your loss is normal and healthy. According to James and Friedman, the steps to grief recovery include: gaining awareness, accepting responsibility, identifying recovery communication (i.e., significant messages that you have not been able to share, such as messages of forgiveness or regret), taking action, and moving beyond loss by no longer carrying unspoken messages or pain. For the purposes of this book, this process has been adapted to:

1. **Gaining awareness** by charting your loss history
2. **Identifying the different types of loss** that come along with the experience of pregnancy loss
3. **Memorializing the loss** through rituals
4. **Working toward integration** by exploring and naming the messages you would have liked to share with your unborn child

In the exercises and sections that follow, you'll walk through each of these steps of the grief recovery process.

Step 1: Gaining Awareness

We often believe that our story of pregnancy loss begins when we first find out we are having a miscarriage. However, an essential part of healing is recognizing that this story of loss begins much earlier than its worst moment. As mentioned, we need to be able to name and understand our reproductive story, or our narrative of parenthood, to move toward healing. Similarly, we need to be able to explicitly name and give space to each of the moments that occurred in our early experience of pregnancy before miscarriage to help us fully understand and gain awareness of the loss.

In the following exercise, you will chart your experience of loss. Begin from however you believe your journey began, whether that was the moment you first found out you were pregnant or the first conversation you had with your partner about starting a family. The purpose of this graph is to help you identify what significant experiences occurred throughout your pregnancy journey that may be affecting your healing process. You may wonder why it feels necessary to chart these events seeing as you are already aware of them. However, many of us were taught from an early age to minimize our feelings or significant life events. Thus, charting these losses and significant moments will allow you to gain the full awareness of your experience that is necessary for healing.

Charting Your Loss History Graph

To complete a graph regarding your loss history, write positive events regarding your pregnancy above the line, like finding out you were pregnant or hearing a viable heartbeat, and negative events below the line, like learning your human chorionic gonadotropin (hCG) levels had dropped or undergoing a dilation and curettage (D&C), which is a common surgery after miscarriage. Determining what makes an event positive or negative is unique to you and can be heavily context dependent. For example, some people may find that it is a positive experience to discover they are pregnant again after experiencing a loss in the past, but others may find it incredibly stressful and negative. As with any exercise in this book, there are no wrong answers here, and this is your journey to uncover.

Your first event on the graph will indicate whenever you believe your story began. It could be when you actually started trying to conceive, or it could be when you had a conversation with your partner about beginning a family. Other events that you would want to mark on the graph include significant positive or negative experiences along your reproductive journey, such as going to doctor's appointments, sharing the news with your family, undergoing any treatments, any successful pregnancies you may have had in the past, and anything else that feels significant to you. If you have had multiple losses, include each of them on this graph.

As you are going through this exercise, your mind may not follow in chronological order, and that's okay. Just let your mind wander without limitation. There is extra space on the page to write any notes you may have. You may also wonder at times if an event feels important enough to include on your graph. As we are about to explore, miscarriage is a multifaceted loss, so please include any losses or events that feel significant to you. A sample graph is provided for you first.

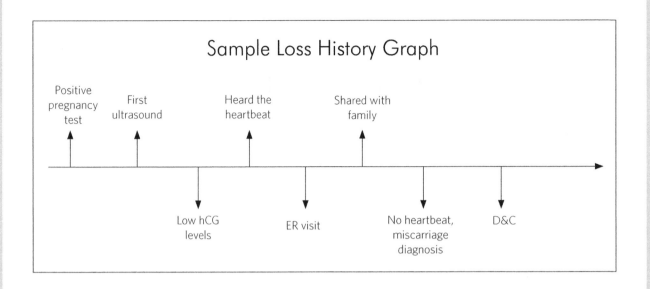

Sample Loss History Graph

Positive pregnancy test — First ultrasound — Heard the heartbeat — Shared with family

Low hCG levels — ER visit — No heartbeat, miscarriage diagnosis — D&C

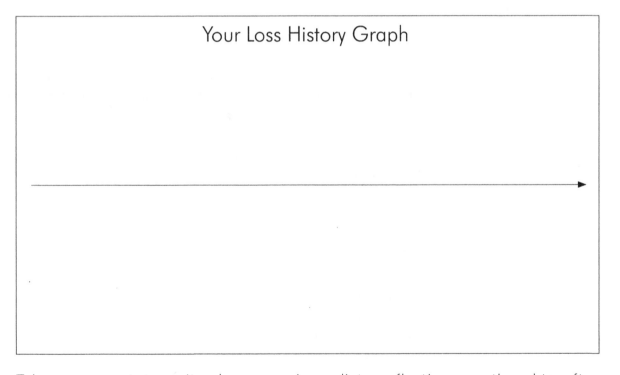

Your Loss History Graph

Take a moment to write down any immediate reflections or thoughts after completing this exercise.

_____

_____

_____

_____

_____

Step 2: Identifying Different Types of Loss

"I've lost my baby."

"I've lost my chance at a first healthy pregnancy."

"I've lost the dreams I had for my child."

"I've lost my chance at becoming a parent."

"I've lost a part of myself."

These are all thoughts that you may experience after pregnancy loss. While some of these thoughts may not hold true forever—particularly if you already have children or are able to have children in the future—in the aftermath of pregnancy loss, these thoughts may feel painfully cemented into your story. Additionally, these thoughts highlight the many different losses following pregnancy loss, including:

- **Loss of one's sense of self.** Our identities and sense of self tend to be wrapped in key developmental chapters, such as parenthood, as well as expectations about our roles that are heavily based on gender norms, culture, and family history. For example, many women associate womanhood with motherhood, leading to questions such as "If I can't be a mother, does that make me a less of a woman?" Similarly, men associate fertility with virility and may think, "If we can't have a baby, does that make me less of a man?" Statements such as these illustrate the impact of pregnancy loss on our identity and view of self.

- **Loss of control and trust in the world.** Pregnancy loss can certainly impact our sense of control and trust in the world. We often feel like we have no control over our bodies after pregnancy loss or feel that we must abdicate control to a medical team—putting our life and our future in another's hands. This can all serve to weaken our sense of agency and trust in the world. Additionally, this loss may cause us to question long-held beliefs we have about the world. For example, the "just world" theory suggests that good things happen to good people and bad things happen to bad people. After a loss, we may begin to question such beliefs and feel at a loss of how to understand and perceive our world.

- **Loss of parenthood.** If you have no previous children, the loss of parenthood is a painfully obvious loss. When many of us find out we are pregnant, we step into the role of parents. We begin being protective and making decisions that are no longer just about our desires and wishes but based on the well-being of this little life growing inside us. We experience a sense of psychological vulnerability as we prepare for this new chapter of our lives. After pregnancy loss, we are left with this vulnerability and all of these wishes and dreams without any place to direct them.

- **Loss of feeling healthy and normal.** After a miscarriage, it is not uncommon to feel like you have lost your "healthy identity." For many, pregnancy loss is the first medical problem or serious concern they have ever experienced. Consequently, going to the doctor and potentially needing to get surgery and don a hospital gown can impact how you view yourself, shifting your view from someone who was "healthy and normal" to someone who is the "sick patient." With any medical condition, including pregnancy loss, there can be feelings of inadequacy, despair, and a diminished sense of self-worth.

- **Loss of the "innocent" experience of pregnancy.** Another important part of pregnancy loss involves mourning the innocent, carefree pregnancy that you always imagined for yourself and likely witnessed in others. There are many exhilarating "firsts" along the reproductive journey (whether this is your first child or not), and the loss of the experience of a healthy, viable pregnancy can be particularly painful.

- **Loss of sexual intimacy and privacy.** After pregnancy loss, and sometimes before, your sexual intimacy may be put under a microscope as doctors ask specific questions about when you conceived, your past sexual history, and so on. Additionally, after your loss, there will likely be a time when you are not able to have sexual intercourse as your body recovers, which certainly can feel like a loss of control over your sexual intimacy. Your desire to be intimate can also be significantly impacted after loss because you associate intimacy with grief, as well as the desire to have children.

- **Loss of financial freedom.** One of the more logistically challenging aspects of pregnancy loss is that it can result in significant financial loss. From doctor's appointments to possible surgeries, the costs of these services can easily add up. It can often feel like adding insult to injury given that not only do you have to pay all this money, but there is no baby that you are going home with after all these expenses. This can lead to feelings of resentment and anger because it feels unfair that you are confronted with significantly greater financial hardship than others.

- **Loss of a sense of belonging.** Parenthood is often seen as a key developmental milestone of adulthood, so when we are no longer able to be parents, we may no longer feel like we belong in our peer groups, especially if most of our friends have children or are trying to have children. As a result of this perceived lack of belonging, we may isolate ourselves even further, creating even more loneliness and disconnection.

Grieving What I Have Lost

Consider the various losses that you just read through. Which losses feel most relevant to your story and your experience? You may feel each of these losses keenly, or perhaps only a few will stand out. Take a moment to reflect on the list of losses and share your reflections. If there is a loss you have experienced that was not listed, describe it here.

_____

_____

_____

_____

_____

_____

_____

_____

_____

_____

_____

_____

_____

_____

_____

Step 3: Memorializing Your Loss

After loss, we often experience a yearning to do something with our feelings—to take some sort of action or to intentionally express our feelings in some way that memorializes the loss. Depending on your specific experiences and phase of pregnancy, you may have had a memorial or funeral for your baby, but that's not always possible and not for everyone. There are other ways to honor your unborn child, such as planting flowers in their memory or having a star named after them. Should you want to plant flowers, gladiolus flowers symbolize remembrance, though you could choose anything that has special meaning to you.

Additionally, you can look to other cultures that have specific rituals or traditions when it comes to honoring pregnancy loss. For example, there is a beautiful Buddhist practice called *mizuko kuyo*, which is a memorial service for anyone who has experienced pregnancy loss or stillbirth. Again, there is no "right" step to memorialize your loss, but if you are needing that, consider a place or an object that had special significance for your pregnancy and consider building a memorial or ritual around that. Use can also use the following exercise to help you consider other ways to memorialize your loss.

Memorializing Through Rituals

Memorializing your unborn child through a ritual can allow you to honor the life and dreams that were lost, which can be incredibly helpful in the healing process. Rituals can have spiritual or cultural meaning imbued into them, or you may want to create your own ritual that feels unique to you and your family. Consider the ideas here while keeping in mind that the only true guideline in creating a ritual is developing one that feels true to you and your experiences.

- ☐ **Name your baby.** Many individuals find that naming their baby allows them to more fully mourn the person who was lost rather than the idea. If you were early enough in your pregnancy that you did not know the gender, you can choose a gender-neutral name or pick whatever name you felt represented your baby.

- ☐ **Plant a memorial tree or garden.** Planting a memorial tree or garden allows you to have a place in nature where you can go to memorialize your child, which can feel healing and allow you to feel more connected to your loss. Additionally, many individuals find it meaningful to plant this garden on the anniversary of their miscarriage or their baby's expected due date.

- ☐ **Wear or make memorial jewelry.** Consider making or buying jewelry that memorializes your loss, such as a necklace that has the birthstone of your baby's expected due date. Additionally, many jewelry companies sell pieces of jewelry that are specific to memorializing pregnancy loss, such as bracelets with your baby's name and angel footprints.

- ☐ **Create a memorial box.** In this box, include all the pieces of the pregnancy that felt important to you, such as the positive pregnancy test, the ultrasound picture, and any other items you want to include, like letters to your baby or pictures of you and your partner during pregnancy. You can visit this box whenever you want to feel more connected with your loss or on anniversary dates (e.g., the anniversary of the miscarriage or the expected due date).

What ritual did you choose, and what meaning does it have to you?

_____

_____

_____

_____

_____

_____

After completing your ritual, reflect on what you notice. Perhaps you felt a sense of peace and closeness to your loss, or perhaps you found it hard to engage and access your feelings as you participated in this ritual. As always, there is no "right" reaction here.

_____

_____

_____

_____

_____

_____

_____

Step 4: Working Toward Integration

Much of grief work is naming the unnamed, and this is especially true when it comes to grieving the loss of a pregnancy. We name the life-altering losses, as well as the more subtle losses, we've experienced along the way. Each of these steps, while excruciating at times, allows us to move toward integrating our experience of loss and grief into our story, thus allowing us to become an active participant in how we choose to move our lives forward. An additional step in this process is naming the messages and wishes you would have wanted to express to your baby. By explicitly writing out these messages, we release ourselves from the burden of carrying these messages inside of us. Speaking from personal experience, the freedom experienced from writing these messages and sharing them with a loved one feels like a massive boulder has been moved from your view, allowing a little more sunlight to filter in.

Goodbye Letter

There are many helpful ways to begin processing your grief following a miscarriage, but one way to start, when you feel ready, is by writing a letter to your unborn child. If you have had more than one loss, consider writing different letters for each child, or write one letter that is meant for all your losses. Include your wishes and dreams for your child, your regrets, and your goodbyes. I have shared my letter that I wrote after my first miscarriage as reference.

Dear my first child,

I never said it out loud, but I called you little seed in my head. While the time you grew in me only spanned months, the dreams I had for you went on for years. I dreamed of big things, like Christmas mornings, birthdays, and family vacations, but mostly I dreamed of the small things that I couldn't wait for, like rocking you in a chair, seeing you fall asleep on your dad's chest, and just staring into your eyes in absolute wonder that you exist and that we get to be your parents. Even the hard things, like sleepless nights, endless diaper changes, and spit-up, filled my daydreams because those things all meant that we got to have you. Your dad and I spent so much time wondering whether you would be a boy or a girl, whether you would have his blue eyes or my black hair, his confidence or my zany sense of humor. (I hoped you had both!) Oh little seed, we already loved you so much. It hurts knowing we will never get to meet you, and I regret not savoring the time you lived in me because I was consumed with so much fear to love you. I regret all the people you won't get to meet. Not just me and your dad, but your grandparents, aunts, and uncles. They were all so ready to meet you. I so wish there was something I could have done to give you a life. I truly would have given you anything. I'm sorry you didn't get that chance at life. You deserved it, and I promise to love you always. I want to say goodbye to you, and I want to promise that you will always have your dad and me. You will always have a family.

Love,
Your mom

Write your letter in the space here:

_____

_____

_____

NOTES FOR THERAPISTS

While grief is a universal phenomenon, it is a highly personalized experience based on each person's story, culture, and perceptions about loss. Therefore, help clients tailor the exercises in this chapter to their own individual experiences. For example, some clients may need help finding rituals that align with their cultural, personal, or spiritual values. As with any other offering in this book, there is no "right" way to navigate this process.

In helping clients work through their grief, it is important for therapists to move between a **loss orientation** and a **restoration orientation**. A loss orientation refers to helping clients process and experience their loss through the act of remembering (i.e., remembering specific moments of their story) and re-feeling (i.e., helping them access emotional reactions and sensations). For example, you can have clients describe their experience of hearing the news about their miscarriage in detail, including the thoughts, feelings, and sensations they experienced in the moments leading up to and after that defining moment. A restoration orientation refers to instilling hope by helping clients integrate the loss into their stories—for example, through rituals or goodbye letters—and finding ways to move forward. This oscillation between loss and restoration is essential in helping clients attend to the necessary aspects of grief work (i.e., expressing and remembering their loss and being witnessed), while also allowing them to balance their energy between feeling and integration (i.e., finding ways to cope and create meaning).

While grief never follows a prescriptive timeline, this is especially the case for pregnancy loss. Oftentimes, the process of natural grieving may be interrupted as an individual finds that they are pregnant again. Whether or not the client experiences this as positive news, the physical and emotional experience of being pregnant again may serve to temporarily eclipse or disrupt the natural experience of grief. Consequently, many individuals may experience what is known as delayed grief, which occurs quite a while after the initial loss. There is no specific time length that marks grief as delayed, but it likely that if clients are still experiencing acute grief six months or more after their loss, they may be experiencing **delayed grief** (Boerner, Mancini, & Bonanno, 2013). Further, it is common for many partners to experience delayed grief as they focus heavily on the reaction and needs of their partner to the point that they suppress or avoid their own experience of grief.

Similarly, the grief that individuals experience following a miscarriage can be further exacerbated by the chronic nature of loss involved in trying to become pregnant again. Many individuals report that each subsequent month that they get their menstrual cycle serves as a painful reminder of what they have lost, which further complicates their grief and causes them to feel "stuck." It will be important to keep this information in mind so you can provide psychoeducation and normalize the experience for clients who may find themselves feeling stuck in their grief.

4

Getting the Support You Need

> "Life doesn't make any sense without interdependence.
> We need each other, and the sooner we learn
> that, the better for us all."
> —Erik Erickson

When we have experienced pregnancy loss, it is common for family and friends to worry that asking about the loss may upset us or unnecessarily remind us of what we no longer have. Yet the reality is, after experiencing pregnancy loss, we *are* thinking about it—very often—so when our loved ones ask us about it, it can be an incredibly supportive experience to share what we are going through. **Remember: There is immense relief in sharing our stories with others.** When we share our story and continue to speak it out loud, we can make better sense of what happened and integrate it further into our narrative. Additionally, by sharing our stories, as well as our fears, vulnerabilities, and pain, we make ourselves available to receive support and compassion, which can be a potent antidote to feelings such as shame.

How much you share of your story and with whom is a very individual decision. Additionally, it can often depend on how you chose to handle the news of your pregnancy. For example, if you made the decision to tell people about your pregnancy early on, then you will also face the task of telling people that you have had a miscarriage. There can be benefits and challenges to this decision. The benefit is that by telling your loved ones about your pregnancy, and subsequently your loss, you automatically have a support group of people who know what you have experienced and can be there for you. This is often the reason many people decide to tell friends and family about their pregnancy before the "safe" 12-week mark: They want the support of their loved ones whatever the outcome of their pregnancy.

On the other hand, sharing news of your pregnancy early on can have its challenges, as you then have to share the news of your loss as well (which is a task that you can certainly outsource to a loved one depending on your comfort level). Once people know of your loss, they will likely, and hopefully, offer you support and compassion, and although this can be incredibly helpful, it can also make it difficult to hold it together at times. For example, I have had many clients who have mentioned that when friends even look at them with compassion and concern during work, it makes them want to burst into tears. As discussed in Chapter 2, healthy compartmentalization is a valid coping skill to use during these times, and having friends or coworkers repeatedly check in with you can interrupt your ability to focus on other aspects of your life.

Thus, in deciding to share your news, it may be helpful to also share some gentle boundaries about how you want others to support you. For example, I decided to share the news of my miscarriages with my coworkers and, while doing so, stated specifically how I wanted them to support me. I shared that I would appreciate check-ins but would prefer that they check in when I was not working or about to see a client because I wanted to ensure that I could be fully present for my therapy sessions. It can be incredibly helpful for both you and the people in your support circle to describe exactly how they can support you. The exercises in this chapter will help you determine what you need and how to ask for you what you need.

It's also important to consider how safe you feel with the people with whom you decide to share and to consider if they can hold the space necessary for you to share. A good rule of thumb is to consider whether or not you want this person to bring up your story with you in the future. For instance, I shared my experience with my coworker (with whom I am close) because I wanted to have a continuing dialogue with her about my experience. I decided not to share my experience with my neighbor because I didn't want to be in the position of her bringing it up to me and having to discuss it further. Ultimately, I imagine most of us have a mix of people with whom we feel safe and can share, while there are other people in our lives we will intentionally decide to keep on the fringes.

What Have You Been Told?

As you explore how you can get the support you need after your loss, it can be helpful to reflect on the messages that friends, loved ones, acquaintances, or coworkers have already told you. It's possible some of these comments have affected the way you are understanding and processing through your experience of loss. For example, some comments—such as "You probably weren't too attached yet, right?"—could have made you doubt your experience of grief and the level of attachment you experienced with your pregnancy. At the same time, you may have received other messages that were incredibly validating and brought you comfort in times of pain.

To begin, list all the comments that come to mind that people have shared with you. I have shared my list here as an example.

Example List

At least it happened early.

This was a part of God's plan.

You are allowed to feel whatever you want whenever you want.

It just wasn't meant to be. What is meant to be will be.

You don't need my permission, but if you need to, you can say no. You can take another day.

Don't worry, everything is going to be okay.

Even if we don't ask, always know you can talk about it.

I still feel upset about my miscarriage a year after it happened.

Write your list in the lines here:

_____

_____

_____

_____

_____

_____

_____

_____

_____

_____

_____

_____

Now go through your list and circle the comments that felt helpful, and cross out the ones that were not helpful for you. Again, while all of these comments were likely given with the best of intentions, there are some statements that will support you in your healing while others may cause further pain. It is also entirely possible that a comment that you find helpful would not be helpful to someone else. For example, "Everything is going to be okay" can feel comforting for some and invalidating for others.

Consider what comments have resonated the most with you. When you are able, say these comments out loud to yourself, and notice what it feels like to hear them spoken again. I encourage you to repeat this practice a couple of times and to pay attention to your reaction. I often encourage my clients to speak certain affirmations or empowering phrases out loud because doing so helps them sink further into their consciousness.

Finally, consider keeping the comments that you found helpful somewhere accessible, whether that be in the notes section of your phone, on a sticky note that you can see on your mirror, or with the survival guide you created in Chapter 2. During moments of pain, I encourage you to come back to these comments and speak them out loud until you feel you are able to receive them.

Explaining Empathy

When we are struggling, we often have this idea that telling others what we need can somehow diminish the weight of what they give us. We may think that they should somehow be able to read our minds and know the exact kind of support we need. I will often ask clients who have this perspective, "Are you more interested in their intentions or their ability to mind read?" If it's their genuine intention to help that you are wanting, read on.

While we can't get support by expecting other people to read our minds, we *can* get support by explicitly letting others know exactly what it is that we need. When you notice that someone is reaching out and giving you the kind of support you've been looking for, make sure you let them know. Couples researcher John Gottman calls this "catch them doing it right," meaning that when you see someone doing or saying something that you need from them, explicitly reinforce this behavior by saying something like "Thank you. I really like it when you ask me, 'What was that like for you?' because it makes me feel like you are interested in what I have to say and are open to whatever I am thinking." This will help signal to your loved one that this is the kind of support you need, which will reinforce their behaviors.

Importantly, other people's ability to support you in times of pain is largely dependent on their ability to *empathize* with your experience. **Empathy** is the ability to put yourself in someone else's shoes and to vicariously experience what they are feeling, thinking, and experiencing. Said another way, empathy involves "communicating that incredibly healing message of 'you are not alone'" (Brown, 2013). It is a skill that takes practice. Providing empathy to another person is hard work because it means that you are exposed to their pain and are sitting with them in it, which can be so powerful. I hope you have had the experience of your loved ones providing you with much deserved empathy, and it's important to recognize it when it occurs because that's the support we need to keep going.

Creating Help Cards

Our support system often has the intention of wanting to help us, but they are not always sure how to do so or what we need. Let's help them (and you!) out by creating "help cards" that outline specifically what you need them to say or do in certain situations. On each card, identify (1) what specific feelings you need help with, (2) what specific phrases people can tell you to help during this time, and (3) what actions they can take that would be beneficial to you. For example:

☐ When I am feeling: *Sad*

☐ I need you to say: *"I am here for you," "You are not alone," and "Tell me what's going through your mind."*

☐ I need you to do: *Sit next to me, bring me a blanket, and hold my hand.*

Create your help card in the space provided here:

HELP!

When I am feeling _____

I need you to say _____

I need you to do _____

Thank you for your care.

After you create your card, consider how easy or difficult it was to identify what you need in certain situations. Oftentimes, we struggle to know what we ourselves need, so just imagine how our friends and family feel! Provide this card to the helpers in your life, or verbally share this information with them, to ensure that you are receiving the support you deserve.

Finding Your Community

"Worst club, best members." This quote is included in many infertility and pregnancy loss platforms and sites, and it introduces the idea that—while we have not asked for it—we are now part of a universal community that has been affected by pregnancy loss. Research tell us that one in four women will experience a miscarriage, which is a shockingly high number. What this also tells us is that there are likely many people around you who have also experienced this type of loss.

While we each have our own unique experience of pregnancy loss, which can be immensely different from that of others, it can still be incredibly healing to connect with those who have endured a similar loss. As many of my clients have described it, there is significant comfort in sitting with those who "just get it." Brené Brown, a social worker, researcher and prolific author, echoes this sentiment in her discussion around shame resilience, where she states that a key aspect to building resilience is seeking out connection and support from those who can offer you empathy (2008). Interacting with others who have gone through pregnancy loss can be extremely normalizing and healing in what often feels like an inherently isolating experience.

Additionally, it is often after loss or other significant life events that we assess our support system, and we frequently discover that we don't have the support we need or that our circle is not big enough to meet our needs. For example, if many of your friends are of similar reproductive age and are either pregnant or have children, it can be very difficult to turn to these friends in times of need. Since creating and maintaining relationships in adulthood can be challenging, it may be particularly beneficial to connect with individuals in the infertility and pregnancy loss community to widen your support squad.

In finding your community, consider your own social network and individuals you may know who have been impacted by pregnancy loss. There are also a growing number of online support groups available through Facebook®, Instagram®, and other social media platforms, as well as specific pregnancy loss support groups. Examples include the organization Share Pregnancy & Infant Loss Support, which offers phone support, in-person support groups, and online communities. Further, consider searching your city for in-person support groups so you can personally connect with others who have navigated this same journey. These communities can hold a wealth of information, such as common physical and emotional symptoms to expect after pregnancy loss, and can offer reassurances that you are not alone in what you are feeling.

Exercise 4.3

Mapping Out Your Support Squad

During times of need, we often struggle to know who we can turn to. Additionally, our needs around support can vary. Sometimes we need a friend to just listen to us and provide validation, and other times we need a friend to serve as our buffer during that baby shower we have been dreading. Complete the following exercise to identify your go-to people for different types of support. You may notice that some friends offer multiple types of support, so list them as many times as needed.

To begin, consider who are the best people in your support squad to turn to and consider which people may have the best of intentions but may not be equipped to support you in the way that you need. For example, you may have one friend who is amazing at problem solving and who supports you in practical ways—like bringing you food or running errands for you—but this same friend struggles to sit with you in your loss and say, "This sucks, and I am here with you." In this case, it may be that you need to provide this friend with more guidance and explain how they can offer you companionship, or perhaps you need to consider other friends altogether who can provide you with the support you need.

Ultimately, you want to have a repertoire of friends who can support you in different ways. That is because, according to David Kessler, a world-renowned grief expert, you can think of your friends' support after a loss as a symphony (2019). Some friends are notes who play in the background throughout the entire musical piece. They consistently check in with you and are there even after the dust has settled. Other friends are notes who only play at the beginning of the song in that they are most present during times of crisis. There may even be notes that you don't hear until midway through the piece when certain friends check in to see how you are faring a few weeks after the loss. You may have some friends who play multiple notes throughout your symphony from beginning to end. Each note is essential to the symphony you will create.

Practical Support: Who would drive you to the hospital? Who would bring you food when you don't have the energy to do anything?

_____

_____

_____

Advice or Information: Who do you feel confident asking for advice or information?

_____

_____

_____

Companionship: Who provides good company? Who would walk around the park with you and share with you in your joys, as well as your sorrows?

_____

_____

_____

Emotional Support: Who can you share your feelings with? Who encourages you and helps you better understand and process your feelings?

_____

_____

_____

Now that you have created your list, use it as a guide the next time you are seeking support. Consider what kind of support you need at the time, and select the friend who can offer you that kind of assistance. If you believe that a friend is capable of offering you the support you need, but they need some guidance in how to help you specifically, give them the help card from Exercise 4.2.

Receiving Support

Although we have moved away from village-like communities, the adage "It takes a village" still holds true. As you may have gathered from this chapter, an essential part of getting the support you need after loss is allowing yourself to reach out and rely on your entire village—even if that means inviting new people to your village. While creating your village is an essential part of creating your support network, an equally important task is allowing yourself to receive support.

A question I will often ask clients when developing their support network is "How are you at receiving support?" Most will automatically answer, "Fine" or "I have no problem asking for help." However, when we dig deeper, we reveal subtle or explicit forms of resistance to taking in the support of others. As a Western society, we are acculturated to an individualistic mode of thinking. We are taught that we need to be able to take care of ourselves fully and that it is not helpful and can even be maladaptive to depend on others. While it is important to be aware of and capable of attending to our own needs, it is just as important to be able to ask for and truly receive the support of others.

Our need to connect with others is evident in the foundational principles of attachment theory, which suggest that when we are babies, we need our parents—who serve as our primary attachment figure—to meet all of our needs (Bowlby, 1969). When we get older, the types of needs we have change, but we still need others to take care of us—to provide us with emotional and, occasionally, physical support. We have a built-in need to connect with others, and Westernized messages that promote complete self-sufficiency, such as "You should be able to take care of yourself" and "You need to be able to fix yourself before you can rely on anyone," can be damaging and unrealistic standards to hold. Instead, it is in the context of relationships with others that we can experience healing. **It is through sharing our story with others and receiving their support and compassion that we can begin to experience relief.**

In order to connect with others and receive the support you need, it will be important to consider how you currently receive support and to reflect on whether there are any barriers getting in the way. Some common barriers to receiving support including:

- **A desire to maintain control.** When you are in the position of *providing* support, you are in a position of control. You may feel empowered, generous, and more in control of your emotions and thoughts. However, when you are in the position *receiving* support, you may experience feelings of vulnerability, which can be uncomfortable and can have unique challenges based on your individual history. For example, consider a woman who has a history of getting hurt by loved ones when she lets her guard down. The idea of allowing herself to be in the receiving position can feel very threatening and incite her defenses.

- **Intimacy avoidance.** As you may have already experienced, asking and receiving support from others will likely bring you closer with others and lead to feelings of emotional intimacy. For some, these feelings of intimacy can be gratifying and nourishing, but for others, intimacy may be associated with loss, anxiety, pain, or even danger.

- **Fear of consequences.** Many people often worry that when they receive support (or any sort of contribution) from others, there will be strings attached—whether those strings are emotional, physical, or financial in nature. Again, past experiences have served to develop or reinforce this belief. For example, consider a child who always received a gift from her parents before they would leave her to travel for the summer. Over time, this individual developed the idea that gifts were associated with loss.

- **Messages about self-sufficiency from early childhood.** We receive and internalize countless messages during childhood about what is "good," "bad," "right," or "wrong." We may have heard these messages explicitly, such as when a parent told us, "You don't need anyone else. You should be able to do it yourself," or these messages may have been implicitly modeled for us, such as when a parent insisted on doing everything themselves and exclaimed, "Nope, I'm fine. I don't need any help!" any time we offered assistance.

- **Familiar roles.** As a result of our experiences in childhood or past relationships, we may have ingrained ourselves to the role of "helper," "caregiver," or "rescuer." When we have been programmed into these helping roles, our focus is on the other, causing us to struggle in receiving the support of others. For example, if someone was the oldest child of four siblings, they were likely introduced to the role of "helper" at a young age, and the dynamics of the family system repeatedly reinforced this role. Consequently, they may find it challenging or even feel like they are doing something "wrong" when they are in the position of receiving.

Barriers to Receiving Support

Take a moment to consider if any of these barriers have impacted your ability to receive support from others. I have provided some examples of my own self-reflections.

Do you struggle when it comes to relinquishing control or have trouble with intimacy because you associate it with loss? Do you maintain a quid pro quo mentality and value self-reliance? Are there messages you heard from your parents growing up or that you internalized as a result of taking on certain roles as a child? Write your reflections here.

Example: When I was younger, I received a lot of messages about how you should not look outside of the family for support. While my family was very loving, they were not very emotionally supportive, so it makes it hard to accept any support I get from others because I'm not used to it, and I feel like I'm doing something wrong if I accept support.

_____

_____

_____

_____

_____

Are there any other barriers not included on the list that have impacted your ability to receive support? For example, past relationships, specific messages you've heard from others, negative past interpersonal experiences, or individual beliefs about asking for help? If so, write those down here.

Example: I keep thinking about this one fight I had with my best friend, whom I've known since childhood. We said a lot of mean things to each other, and one word she used stuck in my head: selfish. She said I was selfish and always thinking of myself.

Maybe there was some truth to what she said, or maybe she was just mad. Either way, it's made me hesitate to ask for and accept help from others.

_____

_____

_____

_____

_____

Now I want you to consider how these barriers have interfered with your healing and in your ability to live the sort of life you want for yourself. Take a moment to consider what beliefs about receiving help from others would be more helpful for you.

Example: It would be more helpful to focus on the feelings of validation and empowerment I get when I receive the support of others. Additionally, it would be helpful to remember that it is okay to accept support from others, just like it's okay for others to receive support when I provide it to them. I can allow myself to receive what I would want anyone else to receive.

_____

_____

_____

_____

_____

NOTES FOR THERAPISTS

After reading this chapter, some clients may realize that they have holes in their support system or in the internal resources they need to cope. When this occurs, take it as an opportunity to help clients build their social network and to work through any barriers they experience in connecting with others. Utilizing the therapeutic relationship in this work can be incredibly healing. For example, clients may be concerned that their friends may be "scared away" or "not get it" if they share the details of their loss, express their emotions, or express their needs. In this case, it would be helpful for you—as another human being hearing their story—to share your experience of hearing their loss and story.

For instance, it is common for those who have experienced pregnancy loss to experience feelings of resentment or hostility toward those who have had successful pregnancies. Clients may say, "I feel so horrible for even saying this, but I'm so mad that she gets to have a healthy pregnancy and I don't." Clients may rush to assure the therapist that they are happy for this other person and feel terrible for even having this thought. This can be an opportunity to share that you are not scared off by what the client has shared and that you can completely understand her feelings. It might even be helpful to encourage the client to give herself permission to say whatever she is feeling without any qualifiers (e.g., "Of course, I'm happy for her and wish her the best") knowing that this is a safe space. Providing compassion and encouragement when clients share some their deepest and most shameful thoughts is one of the greatest clinical interventions we can offer as therapists. However, this approach is grounded in humanistic and interpersonal psychology and may not necessarily fit with all therapeutic orientations.

Additionally, a client's attachment history and attachment style will impact their ability to ask for and receive help. For example, clients with an avoidant attachment style may have learned early on that it is better to rely on themselves to meet their own needs and that it can be painful or even dangerous to allow others to meet their needs. These clients may not feel like they are missing out or lacking support because they are so used to taking care of their own needs. For these clients, it may be necessary to go at a slower pace, allowing them to fully trust in the therapeutic relationship, and to use motivational interviewing techniques to assist them in meeting the needs they do feel are important to them. For example, a client with this attachment style may not explicitly state that she wants support from others, but perhaps she notices that she and her partner have been fighting more, and she wants the fighting to stop. Attending to the client's stated needs will help strengthen the therapeutic relationship and will likely allow a bridge to further explore the client's relational style and history.

On the other hand, clients with an anxious attachment style are preoccupied with fears of abandonment and worry that others will leave them if they express their needs. Individuals with this attachment style often anticipate loss and engage in whatever behaviors they deem necessary to keep their attachment figures present, such as purposefully picking fights in the hopes of prolonging contact with their attachment figure. Unfortunately, this behavior often backfires and leads the other person to withdraw, which then serves to further reinforce clients' anxious beliefs that loss is always imminent and that they need to work even harder to keep their partner around (e.g., more fighting or clingy behavior). For these clients, it is important to work on helping them develop ways to self-soothe, as well as helping them notice and internalize the support they receive from others. Again, the therapeutic relationship can be incredibly helpful as you can process the client's experience of receiving support from you in real time and how much care they are actually able to take in.

5

YOUR RELATIONSHIP
AFTER MISCARRIAGE

> "When miscarriage affects couples, it may stimulate growth, or
> unearth the inability to support each other through troubled times."
>
> — Kristen Swanson

Mourning Together, but Differently

After pregnancy loss, it is not uncommon for a couple's relationship satisfaction to decline, putting them at a higher risk for separation (Shreffler, Hill, & Cacciatore, 2012). This is because pregnancy loss is a trauma, and any traumatic event can disturb the foundation of even the strongest and healthiest of couples. At the same time, the experience of miscarriage does not unequivocally lead to a decay in the relationship. For some couples, the loss may indeed highlight existing fractures in their relationship, but for others, it creates an opportunity to more deeply understand their partner and their relationship.

Whether a miscarriage stimulates growth or stifles it depends on a variety factors, including how each partner reacts to the loss. For example, some couples may struggle following the loss due to differing expectations regarding how each partner "should" be grieving. After a miscarriage, we generally look to our partner as the one person in the world who truly "gets it" in a way that no one else can because they are experiencing the same loss we are. We expect them to be just as sad, bitter, or confused as we are. However, as with any other stressor or major life event, our partner may respond very differently to the experience of pregnancy loss. That is because the manner in which we process trauma varies as a function of our backgrounds, personalities, cultures, and unique ways of viewing the world. Therefore, while both partners will have their own emotional reactions to this loss, this may differ—and differ wildly.

For example, one partner may feel furious and betrayed by her body or the world, while another may just feel devastatingly numb. One may want to share their feelings with any passing stranger, while another may become withdrawn and reticent. Moreover, gender role stereotypes play a role in shaping how we believe men versus women "should" react in the face of difficulty. Women are reinforced for expressing their emotions, so they more often express grief with outward displays of sorrow. Men, on the other hand, are encouraged to hide their feelings and remain stoic in the face of tragedy, so in times of crisis or grief, they are more likely assume the "fixer" role. These contrasting ways of responding can lead to disconnection and conflict as one partner may wonder, "How are you not as devastated as I am?" while the other partner feels overwhelmed and alone in taking responsibility for the family. Though these reactions may appear different on the surface, this is not to say that each partner is not grieving in their own way.

Additionally, while both partners in a miscarriage can certainly experience a sense of loss, their experiences may vary widely. Objectively, the partner whose body miscarried is the one who experiences the physical symptoms of pregnancy and miscarriage and, subsequently, must deal with the physical toll that a miscarriage or surgery has on her body. For many women, growing a baby inside of them also increases the bond and connection they have with their pregnancy. Therefore, the experience of loss can feel more devastatingly tangible as they lose something that was once physically a part of them. Their non-pregnant partners do not have access to this particular aspect of a miscarriage and may need some guidance in understanding what their partner is going through.

Partners may also have different interpretations of the magnitude of the loss. Many women become a mother the minute that pregnancy test comes back positive. They make lifestyle changes and give up things they enjoy for the good of their child, from hot yoga classes to that second cup of coffee in the afternoon. These adjustments may even have ramifications when it comes to their career. For example, a physical therapist may decide to take on fewer patients or may even shift the type of patients she sees to be more protective of her body.

Further, during pregnancy, women may already start experiencing some of the familiar tides of parenthood, such as fatigue and an intense desire to protect this little one growing inside of them. Choices and decisions that they once automatically made now come with a weighted pause as they consider if this would be okay for the pregnancy. Again, these types of choices can span from the mundane, "Is it okay if I have this type of cheese on my sandwich?" to "Is it okay for me to consider this promotion with a baby on the way?"

While many non-pregnant partners may certainly face similar decisions as they consider how their life will change in having a child, many non-pregnant partners have cited that they become a parent the moment they meet their baby in the delivery room. This is not to diminish the emotional experience and attachment they may have in experiencing pregnancy loss, but it highlights why there are often differences between partners in terms of how they respond to and grieve the loss.

While there is still limited research on the subject, LGBTQ+ couples may face additional and unique stressors in their relationships following pregnancy loss. For example, the non-pregnant partner of a lesbian couple may have had already had to confront the loss of not being able to carry the pregnancy (whether this was a decision made out of preference or medical necessity), and the additional loss may further exacerbate any preexisting grief. Additionally, many LGBTQ+ couples may face significant financial, emotional, and physical stressors in their reproductive journey, such as having to use a surrogate and/or relying on the use of assisted reproductive technology, which is often very costly. In these cases, a loss may serve to aggravate levels of stress and pain that the couple was already experiencing to begin with. These additional losses and stressors could understandably lead to negative ramifications in the relationship.

Walk a Mile in Their Shoes

In the aftermath of our loss, we feel so consumed by our grief and pain that it is difficult to take on the perspective of another—particularly our partners. When you feel you are at a point in your healing process to do so, it can be incredibly helpful to consider the experience and perspective of your partner as they endured the loss. Doing so will allow you to better understand their actions, perspective, and ways of responding to the grief.

In the following exercise, you will write your story of loss from the perspective of your partner. Start wherever your story begins, whether it was having a conversation about starting a family, becoming familiar with your partner's reproductive story (e.g., "I know my partner comes from a big family and has always wanted children"), or finding out you were pregnant. Include what you imagine your partner would be feeling and thinking along the way. As much as you can, stay with your partner's experience to fully understand their perspective. Create a title for this story to remind you that this is your partner's story of loss. To help guide you, I have provided an example of the story I wrote from my husband's perspective.

Example: Our Story of Loss from My Husband's Perspective

I'm not much of a planner, but I always knew I wanted to have children eventually. I've been a huge part of my three nephews' lives since the day they were born and often imagined what it would be like when I had children of my own. When my wife first approached me about having children, I didn't feel completely ready, but like most things in our life together, she can convince me to do almost anything. Once we found out we were pregnant, I was happy, but I could tell that my wife was surprised I wasn't as excited as she was. Throughout this experience, I often felt like I wasn't having the "right" reaction. She was often anxious throughout the pregnancy, and I kept doing my best to reassure her. That's been a common role in my life: supporting others through scary times, and it's exactly where I went again.

When we found out about our first miscarriage, my wife was devastated in a way that I had never seen before. I would ask her what she needed and what I could do, but there often wasn't an answer. I just tried to do the best I could to anticipate her needs between fielding calls from our family and friends checking in how my wife was doing. During a lot of our conversations, it felt like I was always saying the wrong thing. I would try to be optimistic, but that usually seemed to make her more upset.

> *Eventually, we decided to get pregnant again, and I was really excited, but my wife was really anxious. I kept trying to figure out how to shift to what she needed. When we found out about our second loss, she was devastated but seemed to be in a better place than our previous loss. I found myself feeling sadder than ever. It's like I was finally feeling everything from the last few months. It was overwhelming and hard, and I'm still trying to understand it.*

While my version of my husband's perspective may not be completely accurate, stepping into his shoes and his story allowed me to consider his experiences and reactions, which I may have not seen or fully understood before.

Now take some time to write your story of your partner's perspective.

Title:_____

_____

_____

_____

_____

_____

_____

_____

_____

_____

_____

_____

_____

_____

_____

At a time when you feel connected with your partner, consider sharing what you have learned from this exercise with them. Again, the point of this exercise is not to perfectly guess what your partner was experiencing, but to offer you the opportunity to further delve into their reaction and to hopefully increase your sense of compassion and connection toward your partner. If it's helpful, you can read the entire story to your partner or, alternatively, you can share some realizations you developed from this exercise (e.g., "I realized that I often told you that you weren't saying the 'right' things or that I needed you to act differently. I imagine that was really confusing for you").

Maybe your reflections or guesses will be spot-on, or perhaps you will make interpretations that were not your partner's experience at all. For most of us, it is not the accuracy of someone else's questions or comments that matter to us, but their intentions in getting to know us. Therefore, your intention to truly understand your partner's experience can go a long way in reconnecting you or strengthening your relationship.

Finally, if it would be helpful, consider asking your partner to write the story of the loss from your perspective. This could be a helpful opportunity for your partner to better understand your perspective, explore any misunderstandings, and deepen your relationship.

Connecting or Reconnecting with Your Partner: CARE

After a loss, we may feel disconnected from our partner. Having differing experiences of loss can serve to compound this sense of disconnection and distance. In order to explore ways in which you can move toward your partner after loss, consider the acronym **CARE**:

Curiosity. Approach your partner with curiosity. Seek to understand what their experience is like without making assumptions, such as "He won't get it because he didn't carry the baby." I often will ask couples in therapy, "Do you want to be married, or do you want to be right?" (You can also amend this to, "Do you want to be in this relationship, or do you want to be right?") If the answer is the former, then use compassionate curiosity to understand what your partner is feeling. While my husband and I certainly had different reactions to the miscarriage, it was through discussions imbued with curiosity that I learned (much to my surprise) how much being a father meant to him and how much he mourned not having that chance, at least for now. I have some helpful questions to guide this discussion in the exercise at the end of this chapter.

Acknowledge. Your process is just that: yours. Acknowledge and respect that your partner may be at a different place than you or may have different needs than you. For example, one partner may find significant benefit from regularly discussing and processing their grief, while another may need some time to distance themselves from the loss in order to feel less overwhelmed. It is important to seek to understand your partner's way of coping and to remember that each person's way of healing is valid. Additionally, consider that, at times, individuals may have conflicting ways of healing. One person may find safety in going to her partner when she is pain, while the other may find safety in retreating to journaling or doing other solo, reflective activities in moments of pain. Each way of healing is valid and likely has a history attached to it given that we develop our own coping styles during early childhood.

Rituals. After a trauma, a couple can experience disconnection and isolation within their relationship. To repair this disconnection, seek out opportunities that create closeness and support. Rituals are one great way to increase connection because they bring both partners together in a shared activity. Following a miscarriage, this ritual could involve journaling together every Sunday or reading a chapter in a book on miscarriage together every other night. Other rituals for connection include doing morning yoga together or having dinner together every night. Essentially, a ritual of connection is a consistent habit or activity that you engage in with your partner that increases closeness and connection. You will have a chance to explore ideas for rituals in the next exercise.

Explore and Explain. You and your partner may vary widely in your experiences of the miscarriage, but even if you don't, it is crucial for you to take the time to explore and explain to your partner what you are feeling and what you need. This can be as simple as telling your partner, "I'm feeling sad today because I got my period and it feels like another reminder of our loss" or even "I'm pissed today and I don't know why, but I wanted to share that with you." It can be hard and confusing to make sense of what is going on in your mind after this loss, but even verbalizing this confusion you are experiencing ("I'm having trouble making sense of why this happened") is enough to help your partner know where you are at. Hopefully, some of the exercises and questions listed at the end of this chapter will help clarify what you are feeling and needing.

Identifying Rituals

Rituals of connection are habits or traditions you adhere to as a couple, such as having technology-free time during dinner or meditating every evening (Gottman & Gottman, 2008). While rituals of connection can be incredibly beneficial at any point in a relationship, they can be particularly helpful in connecting or reconnecting partners after an experience of loss. As with any habit, it is important to do the ritual consistently, whether that means on a daily, weekly, monthly, or even yearly basis (i.e., rituals around holidays).

Consider the list here, and check off at least five rituals you would like to introduce into your relationship. Share your top five options with your partner, and have them choose at least two rituals from your list that you can begin doing together.

_____ Having breakfast, lunch, snacks/coffee, or dinner together

_____ Going to the gym or working out together, including going on walks

_____ Exploring entertainment or cultural attractions in your city

_____ Going on a weekly date night

_____ Doing charity or volunteer work together

_____ Meditating together

_____ Journaling together (There are great journals specifically for couples, such as *A Couple's Love Journal* and *A Year of Us*)

_____ Having designated no-screen-time periods

_____ Learning something new together, like taking a class together or learning something at home

_____ Cooking together

_____ Doing puzzles or playing board games together

_____ Having rituals around hellos and goodbyes (e.g., having a six-second kiss has been found to improve intimacy and connection)

_____ Having rituals around waking up or going to sleep. This can be very important if you go to sleep or wake up at different times.

Write your own ideas for additional rituals here:

_____

_____

_____

_____

_____

Anytime I ask a couple to introduce a new behavior into their relationship, I will follow up by asking if they perceive any barriers to making this change. Barriers could include those that are emotional (e.g., "I'm not sure I'm ready to do this") or logistical in nature (e.g., "I'm not sure we can afford it"). Take a moment to consider any barriers that you and your partner may experience in creating these rituals, and respond with any supports or ideas to manage these barriers when and if they come up.

_____

_____

_____

_____

_____

_____

_____

_____

_____

_____

Impact on Intimacy

After pregnancy loss, it is common for couples to face difficulties with intimacy—both emotional and physical—as they navigate through their grief. That is because trauma can cause us to go inward as we attempt to process and understand our reaction, which can lead to a sense of disconnection with our partner and, in turn, decreased emotional intimacy. Additionally, given that trauma can shake our fundamental world beliefs to the core, we may no longer trust in the safety of our environment, our body, or our partner. Consequently, we may emotionally withdraw from our partner as we attempt to reconcile our experiences and beliefs with our reality. When it comes to emotional intimacy, the challenge after pregnancy loss is that both partners are having their own reactions and are likely expecting comfort and care from their partner while they are both hurting. This can lead to a painful cycle of disconnection in which each partner's inward retreat is viewed by the other as further evidence that they are not safe, thus perpetuating the emotional distance in the relationship and reinforcing the belief that the world is not safe.

In addition, pregnancy loss is a significant stressor that can cause partners to lash out at each other as they move through their grief and pain, which only serves to further disrupt emotional intimacy. Couples will often tell me that they never behave the way they do with their friends as they do with their partner (e.g., "He is the only one that makes me this angry" or "I would never yell at anyone else the way I yell at her"). When this occurs, I will remind couples that it is in our **primary attachment relationship**—our core relationship that we first develop with our parents and that we continue to form with our romantic partner as we reach adulthood—where we let all the parts of our self be known: the good, the bad, and the ugly.

The significance of this primary attachment relationship explains why parents are often baffled to hear that their children are "wonderfully behaved" at school but can be quite disruptive at home. It is only in the safety of the primary attachment relationship—that is, at home—that they feel comfortable fully expressing themselves, even if they express themselves in a way that is quite disruptive. The same can be said of our adult relationships. If my friend tells me, "At least the loss happened early," then I may not say anything and just keep my reaction in check. But if my partner was to make the same response, I would immediately let him know that this comment was upsetting to me. This is because we expect so much more from our primary attachment relationship than we do from others.

In addition to emotional intimacy, pregnancy loss can affect our ability to be physically intimate with our romantic partner. Depending on your experience, you may be told that you have to wait a certain period of time before you can even resume sexual intercourse, and after that time period has passed, you may be required to use contraceptive methods to prevent pregnancy to give your body enough time to heal. While all of this objectively makes sense, it can be incredibly challenging to handle on a mental and emotional level because a lack of physical intimacy may serve to further disrupt emotional intimacy by removing an essential means of connection and bonding. At the same time, many women no longer desire to be intimate after a miscarriage. Before pregnancy loss, physical intimacy likely represented a beautiful pathway to creating a family, but now it simply serves as a reminder of what has been lost.

Further, your body goes through so much after pregnancy loss. You are pregnant for weeks, maybe months, which creates a hormonal roller-coaster and a plethora of new physical symptoms that can all affect the comfort you feel in your body and your desire for intimacy. During pregnancy, your relationship with your body changes as well. You often become protective and aware in a way that you were not before. You may marvel at the miracle that your body is growing this little human inside of you. After a miscarriage, the hormonal roller-coaster continues and a variety of physical symptoms may persist, so instead of marveling over your body, you may start to feel disappointment, resentment, and disconnection toward it. All of these changes may, understandably, have an impact on your desire to engage in physical intimacy.

Although physical intimacy is an important aspect of connection for most couples, we rarely speak about our sex lives or our satisfaction with our sex lives. There are a variety of factors that contribute to our reticence to discuss such a universal and core aspect of our relationships. First, sex by its very nature is incredibly personal, so those of us who struggle to be vulnerable will likely struggle to share concerns about physical intimacy. Similarly, many of us don't want to share our sexual concerns because we fear that we will hurt our partner. Sex is so deeply personal, and we may worry that by sharing our preferences, feelings, or concerns, we will insult or offend our partner. Further, sex is a topic that is often imbued in the taboo. While this is gradually starting to change, many of us received little to no information about healthy sexuality growing up. For many, sex was a bad word in our family, or sex was just never spoken about at all—which has contributed to the idea that sex is not a safe topic to bring up in conversation.

Because sex can feel like such a forbidden subject to bring up in conversation, you may be struggling to find ways to let your partner know of any concerns or feelings you may be having when it comes to physical or emotional intimacy. (And it *is* incredibly normal to have such concerns.) If it feels uncomfortable to do so verbally, consider writing them a letter, or even consider going to couples therapy if you feel it would be beneficial to have a third party in the room to provide support and direction.

Let's Talk About It

When you and your partner are feeling connected, find a comfortable space and time to explore the following questions:

- ☐ What has been your experience with our miscarriage?

- ☐ What have you learned about me after our miscarriage?

- ☐ What have you learned about yourself?

- ☐ What have you learned about our relationship?

- ☐ How has our miscarriage affected your desire for intimacy (in all forms)?

- ☐ What have I done after our loss that you have found helpful?

- ☐ What can I do to support you further?

- ☐ How has our loss impacted your priorities for our relationship?

- ☐ How has our loss impacted your individual priorities for your life, career, and goals?

- ☐ How has our loss impacted your feelings about starting a family?

When you are sharing your responses, try to use I-statements, express what you need versus what you don't need, and stick to describing your own experiences, feelings, and needs. For example, when sharing what support you need, it could be helpful to say, "I really appreciate when you check in with me in the mornings" versus "You never ask how I'm doing." The former informs your partner with what you need while the latter is a recipe for starting an argument. Similarly, when sharing concerns, it is most beneficial to *complain without blame*. It is completely acceptable to voice concerns in your relationship; it only becomes destructive when you share these concerns in a blaming manner. For instance, sharing, "I feel lonely when you go into your study after dinner and would love to spend more time together" is much different than "You never want to spend any time with me and always go to your study after dinner." While both messages have similar content, the former is non-blaming and communicates to your partner exactly what you need, while the latter is a catalyst to conflict and disconnection.

When you are listening to your partner, tune into your partner's feelings, respond with validation and compassion, and ask open-ended questions to better understand your partner and to encourage them to explore further. For example, you can validate your partner's experience by saying, "It makes sense to me that you would feel this way" or "That sounds really hard." It can also be beneficial to use open-ended questions to help your partner feel heard and to encourage them to share more about what they are feeling, such as "This sounds really important. Can you tell me more about that?" or "What was the worst part about this for you?"

If your partner is not open to trying this exercise, go ahead and write down your responses to each question here, and ask if your partner would be open to hearing your responses to these questions. Again, there can be many barriers to vulnerability, and by leading with vulnerability and transparency, we can often encourage those around us that it is safe to share.

_____

_____

_____

_____

_____

_____

_____

_____

_____

_____

_____

_____

Your Relationship with Yourself

Your relationship with yourself, also known as the **self-relationship**, includes the way you view, understand, challenge, and support yourself. Our self-relationship, like many aspects of ourselves, is impacted by our early childhood experiences—specifically that which was modeled by our parents. That is to say that we often model our self-relationship based on our parents' self-relationships. For example, if my mother was an incredibly successful lawyer who excelled at her career and was always attentive to our needs—but she always seemed to have no time for her own needs or even to have any enjoyment solely for her—then I may learn that my role in life is to do for others and that my needs belong on the back burner.

As a disclaimer, parents (and particularly mothers) are often blamed for the follies of their children. However, it is not my intent to blame parents in describing how our self-relationship develops. These patterns of self-development are often a result of intergenerational patterns of family behavior that often go unsaid, are not consciously understood, and are often repeated. Just as our self-relationship was informed by our parents, our parents' self-relationship was informed by their parents, so on and so forth. Thus, in unpacking your self-relationship, consider the ways in which your background and early childhood experiences have impacted your view of yourself. By unearthing these often unconscious ways of viewing and perceiving yourself, you may interrupt unhelpful or even painful patterns of behaving that have persisted for generations in your family.

How Am I Doing?

Many of the exercises in this book will help you deepen your understanding with yourself by encouraging you to support yourself, to gently question and challenge yourself, and to give yourself what you need. However, as with all relationships, you will need to continually work on your self-relationship because your needs, desires, values, and dreams will continue to evolve over time. While there are numerous aspects to the self-relationship, consider the following questions as you examine your self-relationship and write your answers on the lines that follow.

Do you trust yourself? Can you count on yourself to do what you say and to commit to goals and intentions you set for yourself? This doesn't mean that you have to do every single thing you set out to do without fail. It means that even if you don't follow through with a commitment you set for yourself, you are able to acknowledge this and take the time to make repairs, whether that involve making alternative plans or reshaping your goals. What does your follow-through look like? I will often encourage clients to think of their self-relationship as the same kind of relationship they have with a friend and to consider how they approach commitments to friends. How seriously do they take these commitments, and how do they approach their friends if they are not able to show up for them in the way they would want?

_____

_____

_____

_____

_____

What is your attitude toward yourself? How do you respond to yourself when you mess up, do something embarrassing, or make a mistake? Alternatively, how do you celebrate yourself when you do something amazing or achieve a goal you set for yourself? Again, consider how would you treat a cherished friend in either of these scenarios. It can also be helpful to consider cultivating an attitude of curiosity, compassion, and acceptance toward yourself—particularly during times of stress.

_____

_____

_____

_____

_____

_____

Do you consistently practice self-care? Do you have a consistent self-care routine that involves healthy sleep, nutrition, activity, rest, and recreation? If not, what does your routine look like? These are the very basic building blocks needed to sustain a healthy self-relationship. If we consider Maslow's hierarchy of needs, we need to meet our basic needs for safety and health before we can move toward more evolved goals, such as self-actualization (Maslow, 1943).

_____

_____

_____

_____

_____

Have you identified what's important to you? Speaking of more evolved goals, have you taken the time to identify your values and considered how you want to live your life? For some, this may mean setting a structured plan of short, mid, and long-term goals, while for others, this may mean setting guiding principles that support how they want to live their lives. Your self-relationship thrives when it is grounded in values and meaning. What are yours?

_____

_____

_____

_____

Take a moment to consider your self-relationship. How are you feeling about your self-relationship, and are there any areas where you feel you could improve your self-relationship?

_____

_____

_____

_____

_____

_____

_____

_____

_____

_____

_____

_____

_____

_____

_____

_____

_____

_____

_____

_____

Notes for Therapists

Although pregnancy loss can put pressure on existing fractures in a relationship, it can also offer an opportunity to build or rebuild a relationship. The manner in which you help couples work through their relationship after loss is likely to differ based on your theoretical orientation. For example, if you are a solutions-focused couples therapist, then you may direct your attention to helping the couple build coping skills and alleviating their immediate distress. On the other hand, if you are an emotionally focused couples therapist, then you may focus more on understanding the relational dance between the couple and how this is playing out within the context of loss. Regardless of your orientation, it is important to remember that each partner is experiencing grief in their own way, so consider each person's unique contextual characteristics as you consider how best to support the couple.

Additionally, in helping support a couple or individual, consider where the couple is at on their reproductive journey. The very nature of reproductive trauma can be chronic because each month without a pregnancy serves as a reminder of the loss. Even if the couple finds themselves pregnant again, one or both partners may experience conflicted feelings as they become excited over the new pregnancy while still feeling grief for their previous loss. This conflicting reaction can feel even more complicated when each partner is having their own unique reaction to the loss.

The stress of pregnancy loss can also cause early attachment wounds and ingrained patterns of behavior to come to the surface. For example, the miscarriage may unearth a client's feelings toward a past loss that they had long repressed, or a partner's distance may remind the other partner of the dismissive parent they experienced during childhood. Clients may also regress to previous ways of behaving or assume characteristic roles they played within their family systems, such as the "rescuer" or the "victim." When these dynamics emerge in session, work with clients to find the underlying story fueling these patterns of behavior, and help them approach their partner and themselves with curiosity and compassion.

6

Your Relationship with Your Body After Pregnancy Loss

> "I am always learning how to love
> this body and all that she is."
> —Tania Hart

Relationship Status: Complicated

At baseline, many women have a complicated relationship with their body due, in large part, to the messages we receive from an early age of how our body "should" look. Pregnancy can then serve to further change this already complicated relationship with our bodies. When women find out they are pregnant, they often begin to treat their body differently than they have before. They become more protective and more concerned about their body getting all the nutrients, rest, and care it needs in order to nourish this little life growing inside of them. Many women have described becoming tender toward their body in a way they never have before.

Additionally, many women start to adopt habits they would have never dared before, such as introducing vegetables and fruits into their daily diet when they never have before (guilty!) and taking vitamins every day. It's been remarked that the famed "pregnancy glow" is a result of the happiness you feel within your body as it begins this miraculous task. Indeed, many women have noted that the first time they actually feel happy and in connection with their bodies is during pregnancy as they marvel at what their bodies can do and feel more attuned to themselves in a way they have never have before.

Following pregnancy loss, this joyful relationship with your body can move from "Happily in a Relationship" to "It's Complicated" as you no longer feel tenderness and love toward your body, but may instead encounter sadness, anger, disappointment, disgust, or a combination of all these emotions. In fact, a common but often neglected topic following pregnancy loss is the impact that miscarriage has on your relationship with your body. On a physical level, your body is going through an extreme hormonal roller-coaster as it adjusts to pregnancy and then the rapid decline and fluctuation of hormones following loss. Depending on the circumstances of your loss, your body may also be reeling from any medical interventions needed following the diagnosis of a miscarriage. For example, after a D&C, you will likely bleed on and off for at least a week, if not several, which can be both physically and emotional draining because this symptom continues to remind you of the loss.

Further, many changes that occurred to your body during pregnancy, such as weight gain or breast engorgement, continue to persist—for at least some time—following the loss. Many women initially welcome these changes as signs of a healthy pregnancy, but after a miscarriage, these changes can feel like acutely painful reminders of what has been lost. Speaking from experience, I noticed my body changing during pregnancy and joyfully accepted these changes as part of the process of pregnancy and excitedly bought new clothes to accommodate this next stage in my pregnancy. After my miscarriage, it took a while for my body to return to its pre-pregnancy state, and I had to continue to wear the clothes I had bought during my pregnancy. While seemingly mundane, experiences like this highlight the often-overlooked struggles individuals may face in navigating their relationship with their body after loss.

Alternatively, many women mourn the changes in their body after pregnancy loss because it feels like an erasure of the experience to have their pregnancy symptoms disappear and their body return to its pre-pregnancy state. Although the absence of fatigue and breast pain may seem like a welcome experience, for many, the waning of these symptoms can feel like another aspect of pregnancy that they are losing without their control. Many women may even wish to hold on to the weight gained during their pregnancy as reminder of their pregnancy, as well as a desire to maintain some sense of control over their body.

Further, while there have been recent shifts around the idea of women immediately "bouncing back" after pregnancy, this dialogue does not seem to include women who have experienced pregnancy loss. The messages we hear from others, and thus internalize ourselves, is "You just had a baby! Your body needs time to recover." This message, while well-intentioned, discounts the experience of those who were pregnant but did not have a live birth, leading to further shame and self-condemnation about one's body not "bouncing back" after pregnancy. Indeed, the pressure for women to return to "normal" after pregnancy loss is even more heightened as they feel that they do not have the "excuse" of having a baby to rationalize the changes in their body.

Moreover, we often have firmly held expectations about what our body *should* be able to do. Just as I should be able to walk, run, and dance, I should be able to have a successful pregnancy. When pregnancy loss confronts and disrupts this belief, we are often left with anger, disgust, or disappointment toward our body. Indeed, many women cite that after pregnancy loss, they find themselves looking at their body, particularly their stomachs, with all sorts of negative emotions and thoughts. The ambiguous nature of pregnancy loss further exacerbates the negative evaluations we have about our bodies. While some miscarriages may have definitive causes, the vast majority have no clear medical explanation. **Left without any specific cause to blame, we often point the finger toward ourselves, assuming that if there was no outside reason to cause this loss, then it must be because something is wrong with our bodies.**

Mind-Body Connection

There is a complex interrelationship between our mind and body, and in therapy, I often explore with my clients how their thoughts, feelings, and beliefs can affect their biological states. For example, take me before a presentation. I feel quite anxious, and the thoughts swirling around in my brain vacillate from "You got this. You are prepared and ready" to "This is going to be awful. Why do you keep putting yourself in this situation?" As these thoughts get louder and louder, I notice my stomach churning and have to make more frequent stops to the bathroom. Thanks brain, now I'm anxious and my stomach hurts. Conversely, the way we treat our bodies affects our minds as well. Think about how you feel after not getting enough sleep, drinking too much, or eating poorly. I often spend time with clients considering how their sleep, diet, alcohol intake, and other behaviors affect the way their mind operates.

During pregnancy, this already complicated interrelationship between our mind and our body gets even more complex. Before pregnancy, there seems to be a reciprocal, almost linear, relationship between our minds and our bodies. For example, if you only get five hours of sleep one night, you will almost certainly experience some physical discomfort in the form of fatigue, difficulties concentrating, and low mood the next day. This sense of linearity does not apply when it comes to pregnancy. You can sleep for 10 hours and have "pregnancy brain" because you still feel so exhausted. You can eat healthier than you ever have and still feel like you're going to be nauseous at any given moment.

While this mind-body roller-coaster may feel overwhelming, many women embrace it because it is a sign of the life growing inside of us. After pregnancy loss, though, many clients share their desire to go back to "normal." This desire to return to baseline is completely understandable. As humans, we are hardwired to find a place of homeostasis, or stability, in our system. **However, the unfortunate truth that I share with my clients is that we can't go back to that "old normal" because we can't erase the physical or emotional impact that rocked our system in the first place. Instead, we have to create a "new normal."**

Creating a New Normal

Your relationship with your body will likely change after pregnancy. It can be beneficial to identify the changes you have experienced and to use this understanding to inform your "new normal." Use the prompts here to start developing this "new normal." I have included examples from my own self-reflection.

Before pregnancy, my relationship with my body was...

Example: Great! I have always been an athletic person and have enjoyed playing tennis for most of my life and staying fit in other ways, such as rock climbing and running. I definitely took advantage of what my body could do, though I did not always do the best job of taking care of myself. While I stayed fit, I often neglected to drink enough water and was certainly not very mindful of eating enough fruits and vegetables.

_____

_____

_____

_____

_____

_____

After I got pregnant, the biggest changes I noticed in my relationship with my body was...

Example: I was much more thoughtful about the way I treated my body. I was very careful and stopped doing certain activities, such as rock climbing. I also made sure I was drinking enough water and eating fruits and vegetables regularly. Before pregnancy, I would prioritize sending that next email, but after I become pregnant, I started to prioritize making sure that my body was getting what it needed, whether that was a bathroom break or a snack.

_____

_____

_____

_____

_____

From this experience, I would like my new normal for my body to look like...

Example: Taking better care of myself and instilling good habits, such as drinking enough water and having healthy food more often. This experience highlighted how much I tend to ignore my body's signals, whether it is eating enough, drinking enough water, or needing to use the bathroom. I didn't realize how often I was ignoring these signals until pregnancy encouraged me to become more attuned to them. I want to keep listening to these signals just for me now.

_____

_____

_____

_____

_____

Forgiving Your Body

It is completely normal to feel a whole host of negative emotions toward your body after pregnancy loss, including anger, sadness, confusion, and disappointment. **While an important part of the healing process involves acknowledging and making space for these emotions, another essential aspect of healing is finding forgiveness for your body.** Forgiveness is often a tricky term in therapy because it's weighted down with individuals' perceptions and long-held beliefs about what forgiveness means to them. In the context of pregnancy loss, forgiveness does not mean proclaiming that it was okay that this trauma happened. Instead, it involves allowing yourself to let go of any feelings and thoughts that are no longer serving you. In the context of bereavement, we often discuss that when we forgive someone with whom we had a complicated relationship, we can find healing because it allows us to detach and disconnect from any feelings and thoughts that move us away from creating the kind of life we want to live. The same is true for pregnancy loss.

By moving toward forgiveness, we also allow ourselves the opportunity to reconnect with our bodies. While our body was not able to give us the successful, healthy pregnancy when we wanted it to, this does not discount all the many wondrous things our body can and has done for us in the past. Take a moment to consider what your body is allowing you to do, even in the moment. Maybe it is allowing you to sit in a certain position, to hold this book up, and to read the words on this page. Consider what your body has allowed you to do today: You woke up, got out of bed, likely had some food, and maybe even gave your loved one a hug. **There are a million actions that our bodies have done today, but we often let them go completely unnoticed and, in turn, unappreciated.**

Finding Forgiveness

Before moving any further, we need to make space for the hurt, anger, and disappointment you may be feeling toward your body. All of these feelings are normal, yet holding on to them can keep us stuck in our recovery. To help find forgiveness, take a moment to write down all of the reasons you are upset with your body. As you are writing, allow yourself the full freedom to share whatever comes to mind without judgment. For example, many women often feel angry with their body for not sending them a signal that they were experiencing a miscarriage. If this feels true for you, allow this thought and any others to come to the surface without rationalizing them away.

Example: I am angry that I gained weight for no reason. I am upset that my clothes don't fit the way they used to. I am sad that every time I look at myself in the mirror I am reminded of my pregnancy. I am so resentful that my body didn't warn me that my baby was in danger. I am disappointed that I treated my body differently by not eating what I wanted or drinking what I wanted for no reason.

_____

_____

_____

We move toward forgiveness by releasing ourselves from the burden of carrying these perceived injustices and wrongs with us. With that intention in mind, read each of your reasons for being upset with your body out loud, and after each one say, **"I forgive you, and I release you."** If you notice any resistance in yourself as you say this phrase out loud, continue to gently speak it until you feel yourself soften and can fully receive this message. After you are finished saying this aloud, go back to your list and write, "Forgiven and released" next to each reason you gave.

Take a moment to reflect on how you are feeling in your body and write any reactions here.

_____

_____

_____

Finding Gratitude for Your Body

Once you are able to forgive your body, you can more easily find gratitude for it and for what it does for you every moment of every day. Again, your healing is just that: *yours*. If you are at a point where you do not feel ready to find gratitude in your body, that is completely okay. Allow yourself the time to pause and come back to this section when you are ready.

Cultivating gratitude for your body can be helpful at all times, but particularly after pregnancy loss because the mind-body relationship has taken a hit, and women often struggle with feelings of low self-esteem and negative body image. We experience a myriad of physical and emotional reactions after pregnancy loss that make it challenging to appreciate our body, and while finding forgiveness will hopefully allow you to start coming to peace with your body, it is also okay if you are still holding on to some anger or other painful emotions. I will often remind my clients that you are capable of feeling many emotions at once. You can still feel some disappointment with your body while also feeling some gratitude for what your body has allowed you to do.

Body Gratitude Meditation

It would be impossible to count the number of actions that our body performs for us every day, every moment. Yet, most of the time, we are either mindlessly taking for granted what our bodies do for us or actively putting down our bodies for not being "X" enough (e.g., good enough, strong enough, thin enough). Let's take a moment to slow down and reflect on how our bodies show up for us using the following body gratitude meditation created by Debora Burgard (2011), psychologist and founder of the Body Positive movement, which has been adapted for this exercise.

Whether you have practiced meditation before or are completely brand new to this practice, please know there is no "right" way to reflect. I often hear individuals say, "I'm not good at meditating. I can never stay focused." I always reply, "You are not supposed to be good at this. That's why we need practice." And as a disclaimer, I constantly get distracted during meditations, and that is part of the practice. Once we notice our minds drifting, we slowly bring our attention back to the present.

If you feel like you need to pause at any time during this exercise, please do so. Due to the busy pace in which we lead our lives, we often have little time for our minds to slow down and fully experience emotions that have been sitting beneath the surface. When we finally give these emotions the space they need, it may feel overwhelming. Be gentle with yourself and treat yourself with compassion. If you feel like you need a break, allow yourself to gently lower your gaze toward the ground until you feel more centered. Additionally, you may find yourself going through the motions without feeling too much or feeling unable to access deeper emotions. That is okay and normal. Meditation is a practice. Give yourself permission to practice and learn what pace works best for you. I will often encourage my clients to do certain meditations or state affirmations more than once to allow themselves to fully receive the messages within these exercises.

* * * *

Close your eyes and let your awareness settle gradually on your breath, traveling in… and out. Notice your breath coming in and out of your body as your breathe normally. Allow yourself to feel the support of the seat beneath you and the floor beneath your feet. Notice any sensations in your body: places where you may feel an itch, or an ache, chill or warmth, or an emptiness,

93

or a fullness... or even places that seem to have disappeared and feel numb. Just sit with this awareness of your body for a moment.

Take a moment to consider if there is any tightness in your body or any tension. Allow yourself to start scanning your body and releasing the tension in your body. Move around and allow your body to receive your attention. Start with your head, the space between your brows, or your neck... whenever you notice any tension, breathe into this spot and internally say "Release" to allow that tension to dissipate.

Continue this scan from your neck to your shoulders, trunk, legs, and feet. Notice what it feels like to give your body what it needs in this moment.

Imagine the path of your breath, traveling into and out of your body. As it comes in, it warms your body, flowing through your nose, down your throat, and into your lungs. You can imagine that it keeps flowing down, warming your stomach, your pelvis... radiating out into your limbs, all the way to the tips of your fingers and toes. Your breath travels through your body, and as you breathe out, you take any tension that it finds out of your body. Like a warm ocean wave, your breath brings in relaxation and takes away tension. Feel these waves for a few moments.

Now listen to all the ways that you may have experienced a gift from your body lately. As you listen, let your mind create pictures of the recent past, pictures that fade in and out, creating a kaleidoscope of images. Perhaps your body has:

- ☐ *Fought off an infection*
- ☐ *Taken you to the top of a hill*
- ☐ *Stayed awake so you could drive home safely*
- ☐ *Learned a new physical skill*
- ☐ *Rewarded you with the sight of a sunset*
- ☐ *Healed a bruise*
- ☐ *Given you a new sensual sensation*
- ☐ *Gotten stronger*
- ☐ *Kept working despite being in pain*
- ☐ *Expressed a strong emotion through your face or body language*
- ☐ *Defended you from an attack or healed from an attack*
- ☐ *Given you sexual pleasure*
- ☐ *Let you know through pain that something needs your attention*

☐ *Rejuvenated during sleep*

☐ *Allowed you to feel the touch of a loved one*

Take a moment to consider any additional images that come to your mind when you consider what your body has done for you. Allow your day to play out on a projector screen in front of you as you notice each act your body performed for you today.

Notice any feelings you are having as you let these images come and go. Perhaps you are feeling some positive feelings toward your body, and perhaps there are also some angry or frustrated feelings too. Let all of your feelings be present and just notice them.

Think of one thing in particular that you appreciate. It may be hard, but try to allow yourself to land on a specific action or thing in particular that you appreciate from your body.

Let yourself feel the specialness of this gift from your body, the awe and wonder of it. What would you like to say to your "body self"? Create a phrase that expresses your appreciation. What phrase captures your sense of appreciation for this gift? Maybe something like "Thank you for this" or "I appreciate all that you do." Take some time to let this phrase form in your mind. Now say your phrase to your body self. Notice how you feel saying it and how you feel hearing it.

Maybe this is something you could make time to say more often.

Think of a time during your day when you want to be aware of this body appreciation. It could be any time of your day, but pick a situation that usually happens as a matter of your daily routine already. Whatever this time and place is, it only needs to allow you a few moments of reflection.

What is happening at this time of day? Visualize the environment in as much detail as possible—sights, sounds, smells, sensations of touch, temperature, textures, etc. Now visualize yourself saying your body appreciation phrase. Imagine yourself having feelings about saying it and hearing yourself say it.

Resolve to let this situation trigger the thought of your body appreciation phrase so you can feel this appreciation for your body, sincerely and deeply, every day.

Notice the thoughts and feelings circulating in your body. Start to notice the sounds in the room, the seat beneath you. When you feel ready, slowly open your eyes and allow yourself to reenter the space.

★ ★ ★ ★

Now you may want to write about the feelings that came up for you during the meditation. Remember, you may have had powerful feelings or no feelings, or anything in between. There is no "right" set of feelings or images. Try to encourage an attitude of curiosity and respect for whatever your experience is. In addition, include the phrase that you came up with to express appreciation to your body self.

_____

_____

_____

_____

_____

_____

_____

_____

_____

_____

_____

_____

Let's Show That Body Some Love

After identifying the many things your body does for you, consider how you want to show it gratitude. This can be as simple as saying, "Thank you, body" after you finish a workout, engage in physical intimacy with your partner, eat a great meal, or do anything else that your body has allowed you to do. Gratitude can also involve taking the time to develop deeper self-care. Self-care often involves taking care of our body through proper sleep, nutrition, and hygiene. However, in our fast-paced world, these tasks are often done quickly and without much thought. We may take a rushed shower, quickly lather on some lotion, and go to sleep. In showing your body gratitude, I invite you to pause, slow down, and thoughtfully reflect on your body and what it does for you. Consider treating or luxuriating your body in some way.

What can you do to show your body some care? I have listed a few suggestions here:

☐ Intentionally thank your body for how it serves you

☐ Take bubble baths

☐ Treat yourself to some decadent lotion or moisturizer and apply it slowly and thoughtfully

☐ Get a massage

☐ Do a workout you love

☐ Go for a mindful walk

☐ Sit in the sunshine

☐ Use a weighted blanket

☐ Take a long, intentional shower

☐ Do a body scan meditation

Reflect on what your body has done for you and consider how you would like to show it gratitude. You can use some of the suggestions I have listed or create your own plan that is unique to your relationship with your body. Write out your plan to show some gratitude to your body.

_____

_____

_____

_____

_____

_____

_____

_____

_____

_____

_____

_____

_____

_____

_____

_____

NOTES FOR THERAPISTS

The experience of pregnancy can be quite triggering for individuals who have underlying body image concerns or a history of disordered eating behavior. These clients may already have been struggling with the concept of their body changing during the pregnancy, and they may continue to struggle with accepting the conflicted emotions they are feeling following loss. For example, some clients may feel some sense of relief after pregnancy loss because it means that their body will eventually be restored to its original state. They may then feel guilty for experiencing this relief because this reaction runs counter to what they believe they "should" be feeling—namely, sadness and grief. Other clients—who had to work hard to accept the changes happening to their body during pregnancy—may experience some anger or regret at the internal work they have done that is now "lost."

Further, it is often the case that clients' bodies will take quite a while to adjust following pregnancy loss. For instance, many women may still have elevated levels of hCG, the hormone that is produced by the placenta, in their systems for months following the loss. This can be very upsetting because hCG is what causes many symptoms of pregnancy, so many clients will continue to experience pregnancy symptoms months after their loss. This can lead to a complicated mixture of emotions, including anger, sadness, and confusion. Take the time to normalize and validate the conflicted feelings clients may be having about their relationship with their body after loss. Additionally, if clients have a significant history of disordered eating behaviors, it may be useful to seek consultation and consider referring clients to other providers as necessary.

7

SHAME AFTER MISCARRIAGE

> "What we don't need in the midst of a struggle is shame for being human."
> —Brené Brown

After a trauma or significant life event, many individuals struggle with shame, guilt, or both. Although guilt and shame are both self-conscious emotions, they are associated with different internal experiences. We experience **guilt** when we feel like we have done something bad and have engaged in some action that has moved away from our core values. That is, guilt arises when we believe we have *acted* unlike the sort of person we want to be. It focuses on our behavior. **Shame**, on the other hand, moves the focus of the transgression to our self. With shame, not only do we feel like we have done something bad, but we also feel like we *are* bad. Simplistically speaking, guilt says, "I made a mistake," while shame says, "I *am* the mistake." Because shame is directed inward—to our worth as a person—it can be much more emotionally dangerous.

The link between shame and miscarriage has been backed by countless studies and is one of the main reasons individuals who have suffered pregnancy loss stay silent. When it comes to pregnancy loss, individuals often feel shame because they believe they are at fault for their miscarriage, as if there is something inherently wrong with them because they have had this experience. Many of us internalize the idea that having a healthy pregnancy—one that results in a child—is the natural and expected outcome. When we experience pregnancy loss, we then assume that we are somehow at fault—that we have done something that otherwise interrupted this natural process. This belief that we are to blame and that we are somehow deficient because we have experienced a miscarriage can lead to feelings of shame.

Shame can manifest in many ways, causing us to isolate ourselves from others and to become increasingly self-critical. We may begin to castigate ourselves and make character assassinations, such as "I'm so stupid" or "I was so irresponsible." When we shame ourselves in this way, we often harbor the implicit belief that because we deserve to be shamed, then we deserve punishment. This punishment may come in the form of self-criticism or self-harm, or we may even lash out at others as a way to dole out this punishment. I will often refer to the collection of these experiences as a "shame spiral" with clients. It is hard to know when you are in the midst of a shame spiral because it can feel like you have blinders on, and all you can see in front of you are your painful feelings and thoughts. While we cannot rid ourselves entirely of the experience of shame, we can greatly benefit by seeking to understand it better—its symptoms, our relationship to it, and how to move toward healing.

Symptoms of Shame

There are numerous symptoms of shame that can be painful and can negatively impact your functioning. Check off which symptoms you have noticed yourself feeling, and then consider the process questions that follow.

_____ Avoidance of, or withdrawal from, important or meaningful people, places, events, activities, and situations

_____ The use of numbing behaviors, such as drugs, alcohol, food, and various other forms of distraction

_____ Conflict with, criticism of, aggressiveness toward, or shaming of others

_____ Self-defeating thoughts (e.g., "I am worthless," "I am unlovable," "I am useless")

_____ Self-defeating changes in body posture (e.g., slumped body posture with head down)

When did you first start noticing these feelings or behaviors?

_____

_____

_____

_____

What do you do when these feelings or behaviors show up (e.g., ignore them, seek support)?

_____

_____

_____

_____

What could you do when these feelings or behaviors show up that would allow you to feel supported and taken care of (e.g., writing in your journal, meditating)? If you need help generating ideas, consider the coping skills you identified in the survival guide created in Chapter 2.

_____

_____

_____

_____

_____

_____

_____

_____

_____

_____

_____

_____

_____

_____

Silence Perpetuating Shame

For centuries, there has been an implicit, sometimes explicit, veil of silence around miscarriage. This silence acts as an incubator for all sorts of painful feelings, principle among them: shame. Think about it this way: After a miscarriage, we may experience grief, sadness, and devastation. We may have also indoctrinated the message that it is not okay to share these feelings with those around us because it is taboo to speak about miscarriage. Consequently, we keep those feelings hidden in the dark, the proverbial incubator, which allows them to grow and develop from sadness and grief—which are completely natural reactions after a loss—to shame.

When we start to pay attention to the shame we may be experiencing, we start to notice some recurring messages or "tracks" as I like to call them. These messages can be thought of as tracks because they play in a loop, much like a musical soundtrack would, except that the sound of our internal soundtrack involves a cacophony of shame. Shame tracks are those recurring stories our minds tell us about how we are somehow deficient or not worthy. These tracks often include words such as "should" because they imply breaking an implicit rule. For example, the shame track of "I shouldn't be this sad" suggests that there is an implicit rule regarding how sad we are allowed to be following a loss. Additionally, shame tracks include descriptors that question our character, such as "less than" and "wrong with me." Shame has a tendency to play these same tracks on repeat until those tracks become part of the way we see ourselves. Some commonly held shame tracks that women experience after miscarriage include:

- "I'm less of a woman."
- "I shouldn't be this sad."
- "I should have been able to protect my pregnancy."
- "There is something wrong with me if I can't have children."

Often, we are surprised to hear these tracks because we don't consciously realize that we have held such beliefs in the first place. For example, before pregnancy loss, many women don't explicitly state that they equate motherhood to womanhood. However, after they experience pregnancy loss—which serves to test this very belief—that belief rises to the forefront of their minds. Some of these tracks may also be traced to messages or experiences we internalized during childhood, such as cultural norms or beliefs around womanhood. For example, in many cultures, women are not only expected to become mothers, but they also greatly desire motherhood themselves.

There are also certain cultural norms and societal expectations about the age at which women "should" have children and even how many children. Consequently, the minute you reach "child-bearing" age, you may start to receive questions and comments like "So when are you going to give me grandchildren?" or "I bet you are so excited to have children soon!" While these statements are likely made with the best of intentions, they can further reinforce belief that we "should" be able to have children and that there is something wrong with us if we can't or don't have children. Speaking from personal experience, these shame tracks can be overwhelming, isolating, and so painful to hear, especially when they are kept in the dark and played on repeat. We can't stop these tracks from showing up, but we can respond differently the next time they make an appearance.

If there was one technique I could teach someone in therapy, it would be the exercise of noticing and naming. It is so impactful to be able to become aware of the stories our mind tells us, and this is certainly the case for our shame tracks. This is where noticing and naming comes in. Let's say my newly pregnant friend shares how excited she is for me to have kids one day, and just like that my shame track rockets to the surface. Cue the old shame track: "What if I can never have kids? My friend will think something is wrong with me." Instead of battling against this track, I notice it and give it a name.

A key part of noticing is that it's done without judgment and self-blame. You simply acknowledge that shame track—*ah, there you are, I see you*—and then you name it. To come up with a name, I will often ask my clients, "If we were to put all the thoughts, images, and feelings of this experience in a book, what would the title be?" The title of my shame track became *The Motherhood Identity Crisis*. Thus, whenever I notice that particular shame track come up, I simply say, "Ah, *The Motherhood Identity Crisis* is popping up" or even "There she is, *The Motherhood Identity Crisis*, back for a visit."

By allowing yourself to acknowledge and name your own shame tracks, with no judgment and even with a glint of humor, the impact of that track will be diminished.

Name Your Shame Tracks

When you experience a pregnancy loss, shame can act as a character assassin that claims there is something fundamentally "wrong" with you because of your feelings or behaviors. Explore and identify the recurring shame tracks your mind plays on repeat and list them here.

Shame Track 1: _____

Shame Track 2: _____

Shame Track 3: _____

Shame Track 4: _____

Now come up with a title for your shame tracks that you can use whenever one of these thoughts pops into your mind. Remember that the key is to do so without judgment or self-blame.

Shame Track Title: _____

Expose Your Shame Track

Brené Brown uses the term "shame gremlins" from the movie *Gremlins* to describe those recurring stories, or tracks, that our minds tell us about how we are somehow deficient or not worthy. Just as in the movie, Brown also shares that when the gremlins were exposed to light, they were destroyed. Similarly, when we expose our shame tracks to the light of our loved ones, these tracks quiet down significantly.

For example, I experienced the shame track of "There's something wrong with me if I can't have children" on repeat after my miscarriages. When I kept that track secluded in my mind, it just grew louder and louder and more insistent. Knowing the impact that light could have on this track, I finally worked up the courage to share it with my husband. As I began to explain it, I experienced Brown's theory coming to life: As I exposed my shame gremlin to the light, I became aware of how ludicrous this story sounded. I didn't criticize myself for having this story in my head but allowed myself to really hear the inaccuracy of it while experiencing the love and support of my husband.

And just like that, this track, which had consumed hours of my time and so much energy, evaporated.

Expose Your Shame Tracks

After you have identified your dominant tracks, choose a loved one with whom you feel safe, and share these tracks out loud with them. Allow yourself to notice your reaction in speaking these stories out loud, and consider the response of your loved one. After you share your shame tracks with your loved one, consider the following questions to help you process your experience.

What did it feel like to speak your shame track out loud?

_____

_____

_____

_____

How did you experience your loved one's reaction?

_____

_____

_____

_____

If your loved one had been in the same situation as you and was having the same thoughts and feelings, what would you tell them?

_____

_____

_____

_____

The next time this track comes up, notice it and name it explicitly, and recall your loved one's reaction.

Combating Shame with Self-Compassion

Research and clinical experience has shown time and time again that compassion is the antidote to shame. In particular, neuroscience research has shown that when shame gets stuck in our neural circuitry, we can proactively repair it with exercises in self-compassion and self-empathy (Jankowski & Takahashi, 2014). When we feel shame, our body responds as if it is in danger, activating the fight-flight-freeze response and resulting in the familiar release of stress hormones, such as cortisol and adrenaline. When these experiences of shame are prolonged or repeated, they get imprinted into our brain via well-grooved neural pathways, which are reinforced across time, leading to the continued release of stress hormones. This can increase blood pressure and cause fatigue in the short term, as well as have more serious consequences, such as depression, in the long term.

Self-compassion exercises serve to interrupt this familiar neural circuitry and instead trigger the release of the hormone oxytocin, which is known for creating feelings of trust, peace, safety, generosity, and connectedness (Engel, 2013). Over time and with repeated practice, our brain's capacity for neuroplasticity—that is, its natural ability to rewire itself—allows for the creation of new neural pathways that are associated with kindness and caring instead.

Cultivating self-compassion begins by connecting with our suffering. Understandably, most of us shy away from focusing on our own pain, and we may engage in avoidance or numbing behaviors to distract ourselves from our wounds. However, by ignoring our wounds, we are unable to heal the emotions that accompany that wound, including shame. ACT uses the metaphor of attempting to hold a volleyball under water to illustrate the difficulties in attempting to avoid our suffering. We can continue to hold the volleyball under the water and use up precious energy and attention while doing so, but eventually, our arms will get tired. We will be unable to continue holding the ball under water, and it will inevitably rise to the surface. Similarly, while we can ignore our suffering for a time, those feelings will eventually come to the surface.

In contrast to stifling our shame, we can use self-compassion to intentionally acknowledge those feelings and extend kindness to ourselves in the process of doing so. Instead of trying to change those feelings or fight against them, we simply nonjudgmentally acknowledge their existence without getting caught up in them. In addition, self-compassion involves treating ourselves with warmth and kindness, even in times of defeat or failure, and even when we are suffering. When we exhibit self-compassion, we treat ourselves with the same kindness, care, and compassion we would extend to a loved one. Self-compassion also involves the recognition that we all experience shame and that we are not alone in our struggles (Neff, 2011). Feelings of inadequacy and imperfection are a universal aspect of the human existence. When we realize that we all share this common humanity, it allows us to feel less isolated and alienated from others.

Self-Compassion Letter

Compassion can do wonders to manage our shame. This self-compassion exercise is adapted from the wonderful Dr. Kristin Neff (2009), a well-known researcher, writer, and all-around self-compassion guru. In this three-part exercise, you will write yourself a self-compassion letter so you can find greater comfort and acceptance. I have included the letter I wrote when completing this exercise as an example.

Part 1: Begin by writing about the specific situation or triggers that caused you to feel inadequate or bad about yourself. What emotions come up for you when you think about this aspect of yourself? Try to just feel your emotions exactly as they are—no more, no less—and then write about them.

Part 2: Now think about an imaginary friend who is unconditionally loving, accepting, kind, and compassionate. Imagine that this friend can see all your strengths and all your weaknesses, including the aspect of yourself that you have just been writing about. Reflect upon what this friend feels toward you and how you are loved and accepted exactly as you are, with all your very human imperfections. This friend recognizes the limits of human nature and is kind and forgiving toward you. In their great wisdom, this friend understands your life history and the millions of things that have happened to create you as you are in this moment. Your perceived inadequacy is connected to so many things you didn't necessarily choose: your genes, your family history, and your life circumstances—all of which are outside of your control.

Now write a letter to yourself from the perspective of this imaginary friend—focusing on the perceived inadequacy for which you tend to judge yourself. What would this friend say to you about your "flaw" from the perspective of unlimited compassion? How would this friend convey the deep compassion they feel for you, especially for the pain you feel when you judge yourself so harshly? What would this friend write in order to remind you that you are only human, that all people have both strengths and weaknesses? And if you think this friend were to suggest that you make possible changes, how would these suggestions embody feelings of unconditional understanding and compassion? As you write to yourself from the perspective of this imaginary friend, try to infuse your letter with a strong sense of your friend's acceptance, kindness, care, and desire for your health and happiness.

Part 3: After writing the letter, put it down for a little while. Then come back and read it again, really letting the words sink in. Feel the compassion as it pours into you, soothing and comforting you like a cool breeze on a hot day. Love, connection, and acceptance are your birthright. To claim them you need only look within yourself.

Here's what this exercise looked like for me:

Part 1: *I started to feel bad about myself when I even imagined telling my friends that I would not be able to plan their baby shower. I felt guilty and weak, and I wondered why I was not able to push my own feelings to the side to focus on what was such a huge and joyous event in their lives. I also felt sad, hopeless, and disconnected when I was at my friends' baby shower and I saw their other friends reaching toward my friends' pregnant bellies with wonder and excitement. I realized I had never once touched their pregnant bellies after my miscarriage and was immediately filled with disappointment, grief, and shame.*

Part 2: *Dear Sunita, I can hear how much pain you have been in. I know it hurts to not be there for your friends in the way you want to, and I know you wish you had this superhuman ability to push your emotions and the last few months aside and just pretend that everything is okay. I want you to know that it is okay that you are not okay. You have been through loss, pain, and trauma in the last few months. I know there have been times you have struggled to make it through the day, through work, through conversations with friends, and that's okay because you have been through so much.*

You can be excited for your friends and still feel grief and loss for yourself. It's so absolutely human and natural to dread going to an event that is baby-centered when I know it's the last thing you want to think about, and that's okay. It's okay that you wish you could put the rest of the world on pause for a little while longer until you have some more time to grieve. It's okay that you dread going to that party, that you aren't as excited for your friends as you wish you could be, and it's okay if you go and just make it through the party because that is a lot right now. What I wish for you is that you offer yourself some grace and compassion and that you can see how strong you are. I wish that anytime those feelings of sadness, anger, or disappointment come up when you see a pregnant person or anything baby-related, that you can acknowledge those feelings and let yourself just notice them without fighting them, without judging them, and then you can tell yourself like I'm telling you now: It's okay to feel that way. There is no right way to feel after a loss. It's okay that you are not okay right now.

Love,
Sunita
(Also, Alex, who was the compassionate friend I was picturing)

Now take some time to write your own self-compassion letter in the space here.

_____

_____

_____

_____

_____

_____

_____

_____

_____

_____

_____

_____

_____

_____

_____

_____

_____

_____

_____

_____

_____

_____

_____

Shame and Your Values

As you become more flexible with your shame, it becomes possible and can be very helpful to explore your values as a means of responding to any lingering feelings of shame and guiding your path forward. ACT defines our values as activities or concepts that give our life meaning. Our values can be thought of as our compass to help us make choices based on the directions in which we want our lives to go. Thus, when a painful feeling comes up, such as shame, you can notice it, name it, and then use your values as a compass to determine where you want to move next. For example, if my previous shame track of "There's something wrong with me if I can't have kids" comes up, I would notice it, name it, and then move toward my identified values of learning and connection. This could look like intentionally turning toward a loved one around me (if I was moving toward connection) or becoming curious about the experience of shame and deciding to listen to a podcast to better understand it (if I was leaning into learning).

Other common values that individuals may identify include their career, faith, growth, travel, and altruism. These values can provide a sense of direction when individuals are feeling consumed by feelings of shame following loss. For instance, if I had the shame track "I should have been able to protect my baby" running through my mind, I could acknowledge this track and then encourage myself to reflect on my value of altruism. I could consider what altruism means to me and decide to direct this value outward in the form of volunteer work or service to my community. Additionally, our values not only provide us direction, but they also allow us to gain a broader perspective on our view of ourselves and what truly matters to us. For example, perhaps I feel shame after having a miscarriage because I believe my worth is dependent on my ability to have children. Again, I could turn toward my values compass, and if my career is one of my values, this could encourage me to more deeply consider what I choose my worth to be.

The Life Compass*

Use the following table to help you identify your values. First, write a few key words about what is important or meaningful to you in each domain of life: What sort of person do you want to be? What sort of personal strengths and qualities do you want to cultivate? What do you want to stand for? What do you want to do? How do you ideally want to behave? If a domain seems irrelevant to you, that's okay. Just leave it blank. If you get stuck on a domain, then skip it and come back to it later. And it's okay if the same words appear in several or all domains: This helps you identify core values that cut through many domains of life.

Next, rate how important these values are to you at this point in your life (1 = not important, 10 = extremely important). It's okay if several domains all have the same score. Finally, rate how effectively you are living by these values right now (1 = not at all, 10 = living by them fully). Again, it's okay if several domains all have the same score.

Here's what my table looked like after I filled it out:

Domain	What's important to you in this domain of life?	How important is it to you? (1-10)	How effectively are you living this? (1-10)
Intimate Relationships	*Being a loving, compassionate, and patient partner who is continuously seeking to grow and learn*	10	8
Family Relationships	*Being patient, loving, and warm with family and being grateful for my time with them*	10	6
Social Relationships	*Being consistent, kind, and honest in my friendships*	9	7
Personal Growth	*Continuously being curious and working to learn more about myself; Not allowing myself to fall into too rigid of a routine*	8	8
Leisure	*Engaging in hobbies and allowing them to be non-productive; Allowing myself to play and have time without goals*	7	7
Spirituality	*Allowing myself time to meditate and connect with my values on a deeper level*	9	6
Career	*Consistently looking for ways to grow and learn while also allowing for gratitude in what I get to do each day*	10	8
Health	*Exercising, eating healthy, getting enough sleep, and treating my body with kindness and gratitude*	8	5
Community and Environment	*Making an impact in my community through big actions (volunteer work, presentations) and small actions, such as a connecting with others and spreading kindness*	10	7

* Adapted from Russ Harris's (2013) ACT-based values exercise

Now see if you can give it a try:

Domain	What's important to you in this domain of life?	How important is it to you? (1-10)	How effectively are you living this? (1-10)
Intimate Relationships			
Family Relationships			
Social Relationships			
Personal Growth			
Leisure			
Spirituality			
Career			
Health			
Community and Environment			
Other:			

---

* Adapted from Russ Harris's (2013) ACT-based values exercise

Consider what you have written. What does this tell you about...

What is important in your life?

Example: I noticed these words come up again and again: gratitude, curiosity, learning, and kindness. I always knew that learning and curiosity were important to me, but I never realized how essential I find gratitude and kindness to be. I think I take those values for granted.

_____

_____

_____

_____

What you are currently neglecting?

Example: I think I could take more time to focus on gratitude and to consider ways that I could spread kindness more consistently. This doesn't have to be in huge ways, like taking on new projects, but even taking that extra moment to consider what I could do to make someone's day a little lighter would fill me up as well.

_____

_____

_____

_____

_____

* Adapted from Russ Harris's (2013) ACT-based values exercise

NOTES FOR THERAPISTS

As you help clients explore and identify their feelings of shame, it will be important to understand these emotions within the unique context of each client's background. For many, shame may be tied to cultural underpinnings, such as specific expectations about what a person *should* be or *should* do, which can then fuel the development of clients' shame tracks. For example, in some Latin American cultures, a woman's value is tied to her ability to have children. This cultural expectation is often explicitly or implicitly reinforced throughout childhood. If a client from this background is unable to have children, she may begin to question her worth and develop feelings of shame around her loss (e.g., "I am worthless because I cannot have a child. There is something wrong with me").

Therefore, it may be beneficial to explore the origins of certain shame tracks that clients play on repeat. Consider how the client learned those tracks, and see if they agree with the beliefs that underlie these tracks. After undercovering the origins of my clients' shame tracks, I will often ask them, "Are you okay with this belief?" Oftentimes, the answer is no, and we move toward developing a belief that they can now consciously choose as an adult.

As a note, some theoretical approaches, such as ACT, don't support the need to identify the origins of shame tracks. ACT is a present-centered, highly experiential approach that focuses more on the second question I pose to my clients ("Are you okay with this belief or shame track?") and moves from there. As with much of therapy, there is no "absolutely correct" way of exploring shame, and it will depend on the needs of your client, as well as your own theoretical background.

Some clients may struggle to identify their shame tracks because they are not familiar with the practice of intentionally noticing and identifying their thoughts. They may even say that they are not aware of any thoughts floating around in their head. In these cases, I suggest clients pay attention to the sensations in their body. Shame is a powerful emotion that is often associated with accompanying physical sensations, such as tightness in the chest, a churning stomach, or a slumped posture. Encourage clients to pay attention when they notice these sensations or other uncomfortable bodily sensations showing up and to note what they were thinking and doing at the time. You can assign clients this task for homework to help them explore their shame tracks and develop greater awareness of their internal states.

8

MOVING FORWARD, NOT ON

"Life determines the plot. But you write the story."
—Unknown

Let's take a moment to unpack the title of this chapter. There is no "moving on" or "moving past" after loss. A significant life event and trauma has interrupted your life and likely the lives of your closest loved ones, and it will take time to process and heal. Moving forward then means allowing this experience to take some space in your life, integrating it into your story, and then deciding how to move forward in a way that is congruent with creating the kind of life you want to build.

Many of you may be familiar with the stages of grief developed by Elizabeth Kübler-Ross (2005), an expert on death and dying. They include depression, anger, bargaining, denial, and acceptance. Throughout her work, Kübler-Ross made groundbreaking insights into how we experience death and reduced the stigma in discussing the universal experience of loss. The applicability of these stages have come under scrutiny in recent years because many believe they suggest a prescriptive way of experiencing grief and can cause people to feel as if they are not grieving "correctly" if they do not cycle through all the stages. However, Kübler-Ross originally developed these stages to describe the process patients go through as they confront their *own* diagnosis of a terminal illness. The stages were only later applied to the experience of those who have lost a loved one, who seemed to undergo a similar process after their loss.

Therefore, it is perfectly normal to not experience all the stages of grief included in Kübler-Ross's model. We may even cycle through the same stages repeatedly and out of order. For example, a woman may experience denial and anger as she does everything she can to avoid feeling the pain of her loss, only to eventually fall into a place of depression. Alternatively, another woman may first experience depression and then shift into a place of denial as she finds her emotions too overwhelming to handle. The chronic nature of the reproductive journey can further complicate the unfolding of these stages because a woman may experience acceptance, but after becoming pregnant and miscarrying again, she may fall back into depression as she finds herself remembering her first loss and then become hopeless of ever having a healthy pregnancy.

In addition, new research has introduced a sixth stage of grief called **meaning making,** which can include, but is not limited to, finding gratitude for the time you had with your loved one, finding ways to commemorate or honor your loved one, realizing the brevity and value of life (and using that realization as a motivator to make life changes), feeling changed by having experienced loss, and creating something of meaning for others. My experience of meaning making following my losses were varied and still continue to unfold to this day. For example, I became more connected with friends to whom I had previously only been tangentially connected and who also had a history of miscarriage. We bonded over our shared experiences, and our relationship deepened in a profound way that has allowed us to become incredibly close. Similarly, during the time I was pregnant, I found myself reflecting on the importance of family in a way I never had before. I not only took the time to consider the kind of family I dreamed to build with my husband, but I also reflected on the family I was born into and my gratitude for each and every moment with them. While I wish that my losses would never have occurred, I can still be grateful for the opportunities and insights my grief and experiences have given me.

As you consider how to find meaning in your loss, it is important to keep some guidelines in mind:

- **Meaning is relative and personal.** Your relationship to your loss will not be the same as your partner's or anyone else who has experienced this kind of loss. Allow your loss to be just that: *yours*.

- **Meaning takes time.** Grief moves through phases. We may initially experience anticipatory grief as we learn of the possibility of pregnancy loss. We then experience acute grief after hearing the news and being in the thick of our pain, which will fade in intensity over time. These phases are not a map but, rather, offer an idea of some of the experiences you may face and suggest that moving toward meaning making will take time.

- **Meaning does not equal understanding.** When we allow ourselves to find meaning in our suffering, it does not mean we agree with the loss or understand it. After pregnancy loss, we often hear phrases such as "It just wasn't meant to be." This phrase may resonate for some people, but many others find such a sentiment invalidating and hurtful. Thus, meaning making does not mean that we reach an understanding of why our loss happened but *that we choose to find meaning in our suffering.*

- **Meaning doesn't negate the loss and isn't worth the cost of losing someone.** Loss is never worth the meaning we experience after it. The hero's journey often depicted in books and movies suggests that we need to experience a significant and often devastating trial in order to find greater purpose. This is not true, and while we may find greater meaning after loss, it does not negate the pain we experienced or make it "worth it."

- **Only you can find your own meaning.** No one else can tell you how to make meaning out of your loss. No one can tell you how this experience has changed you, and no can define for you the hope, meaning, and depth that you may or may not get out of experiencing a miscarriage.

Meaning Making

To help you begin defining your experience of meaning making, consider the following prompts. Allow yourself to write freely without filtering or monitoring your words. Meaning takes time, so if there is one question you feel unable to answer, allow yourself to come back to it when you are ready.

What could the loss not touch?

Example: The loss did not touch my core values, which are learning and connection. While it was hard to lean into those values at times, they did serve as an anchor for me when I was feeling adrift. I intentionally made plans to spend time with friends and family even when I didn't feel like it because I knew I would find it energizing afterward, and I signed up for an online course in couples therapy because I knew the healthy distraction of learning would be nourishing for me.

_____

_____

_____

_____

How can I recognize my survival strength?

Example: I can recognize my strength in small moments and small actions. I was strong when I got out of bed this morning, I was strong when I went to work, and I was strong when I shifted my focus from myself to my partner so I could help him through his pain. Even though each of these steps took a ton of energy, I feel stronger for it.

_____

_____

_____

_____

What do I still have control over?

Example: I have control over how I show up—of how I choose to grieve, talk about my loss, or not talk about it. I have control over what path I choose next, and I have control over what actions I choose to take each day. I have control over how I choose to spend my energy, and today that will be going for a run.

_____

_____

_____

What meaning can I find from this experience that can heal me and honor the pregnancy?

Example: This experience allowed me to develop and deepen relationships with friends in a way that I didn't know was possible. There is one particular friend who comes to mind, who has also had a miscarriage, and she and I have become so close over the last years mourning and commiserating over our losses. She is now pregnant and rather than being upset by this, I find supporting her to be healing for me.

_____

_____

_____

What parts of me came alive during pregnancy? How can I continue to foster and grow these parts?

Example: What came alive for me during my pregnancy was my capacity to care for myself physically. While I am regularly active, I certainly neglected other parts of my physical care before pregnancy, including ensuring I was getting proper nutrition, getting enough sleep, and so forth. My experience of pregnancy has encouraged me to maintain the habits I began during pregnancy for myself this time.

_____

_____

_____

Redefining Fertility and Regaining Control After Pregnancy Loss

In the infertility community, a "rainbow baby" refers to a baby you have after experiencing infertility or pregnancy loss. It's thought that the baby is your rainbow after the storms you've endured. This is a beautiful sentiment, and there are numerous stories of courage and resilience in which individuals share how they have endured significant physical, emotional, and, often, financial stress to finally have their rainbow baby.

While it is important to highlight these stories of hope that can follow pregnancy loss, it is just as important to emphasize that the path to your "rainbow" does not always need to include having a baby at the end. After someone has experienced miscarriage or infertility, there is often an assumption from loved ones, friends, and maybe even ourselves that we must try to have a baby again—and soon—whether that means trying to conceive again, utilizing assisted reproductive technology, or exploring other options, such as adoption.

After my miscarriages, I was often asked when my partner and I were going to try again and told "don't give up" when we started to wonder whether we wanted to continue trying to have children. While these words of support were given with the best of intentions, they also assumed that there is only one "right" path after pregnancy loss: namely, to keep trying to have a baby. If this is the path you and your partner want to pursue, that is amazing. However, it's important to take a moment to reflect and to consider what next step you want to choose for yourself.

The keyword here being—*choose*. Pregnancy loss has a way of taking away our ability to choose. It can feel like control or agency is taken away from you after a miscarriage. You experience a painful emotional and physical trauma without any say in the matter. Additionally, certain choices in your life, such as when to have a baby or how to have a baby, may become dependent on forces outside of your control, such as medical factors or even financial limitations. Consequently, pregnancy loss can leave individuals feeling disempowered and helpless (Wojnar et al., 2011). The following exercise will support you in recognizing your agency after loss so you can find your own unique rainbow.

Find Your Rainbow

The "rainbow" is considered your refuge after the storm, and while that can mean a baby, it can also mean a host of other paths. One way to identify your rainbow is to consider the word *fertility*. While we often limit this concept to the ability to conceive children, fertility refers to richness, fruitfulness, and generativity. Thus, having a fertile life can mean creating a life that has meaning, worth, and richness that is not dependent on the ability to have children but, rather, on cultivating a life that embodies *your* definition of fertility.

In finding your definition of fertility, it is helpful to consider your values. As mentioned in Chapter 7, values are defined as activities or concepts that give our life meaning, such as learning, connection, or family. Your values can be thought of as your compass to help you make choices based on the directions in which you want your life to go. Consider the values you identified from the exercise in Chapter 7, and keep them in mind as you explore the following reflection questions.

When do you feel grateful or appreciative? For what?

_____

_____

_____

_____

What gives you a sense of pride, achievement, mastery, and control?

_____

_____

_____

_____

What inspires you? What infuriates you?

_____

_____

_____

_____

When do you feel you're living life your way? Doing what?

_____

_____

_____

_____

Your answers to these questions will provide valuable information regarding the relationships, activities, beliefs, goals, and desires that are most important to you. For example, perhaps you will learn that you feel most inspired when you are in leadership positions or mentoring others, or perhaps you'll find that you feel most appreciative of opportunities when you were able to travel and experience other cultures. These insights can be used to help guide you in identifying your values and using these values as a compass to consider what choice you would like to take next.

It's important to note that our values and our dreams are not static. Perhaps, based on your current values, you decide to choose the path of seeking to build your family. Or maybe you decide that what you need right now is to focus on your current relationships or your passion for writing. My intention here is not to advocate for any specific dream but to share that the path to finding your rainbow or living a fertile life is not limited to one road. Pregnancy loss can leave us feeling adrift without a say in what our future holds. Thus, it is so important to acknowledge and hold on to the power you do have in your life whether that means pursuing the family you dream of or taking the time to consider what other beautiful paths your life could take.

Using Your "Why" to Guide Your "How"

One of my favorite concepts to share with clients is: "We are going to use your *why* to inform your *how*." This notion is incredibly important in creating a life that aligns with your wishes, hopes, and values. Your "why" refers to your purpose, your mission, and (again with my favorite word) your values. Through some of the earlier exercises, you have now identified your "why," and you can use that why to inform your "how," which refers to the specific steps you will take and goals you will define. For example, if you have identified that your values and purpose lie in the impact you can create for others, then maybe you will decide to find ways to volunteer and provide support for your community. Or if you decide that your values lie in your relationship, then perhaps you will decide that it would be helpful for you and your partner to spend some intentional time focusing on your connection and your future. Additionally, if you find that your values lie in creating a family, then perhaps you start deciding which path to that destination feels most aligned with your mission.

In defining your "how," it's important to acknowledge that the "how" you choose now may not be your first choice or the path you always imagined for yourself. Many of us after loss have trouble identifying a path forward because we always dreamed of our lives following a certain trajectory (i.e., our reproductive story). You may experience a mixture of emotions to defining this new path that is different from what you always imagined for yourself. Take a moment to grieve that loss, and allow yourself to choose how you want to move forward in a way that is consistent with the kind of life you want to create. **I am not asking you to be optimistic about your loss, but I will ask you to be optimistic about the future you are creating.**

DEFINING YOUR "HOW"

Let's start defining what your unique "how" is going to look like. Consider and respond to the following prompts to support you in creating your path forward. I will also ask you to consider any barriers to reaching your goals, as well as supports that could help you if confronted by said barriers.

Based on previous exercises and self-reflection, my "why" tells me that I want to focus on...

Example: After focusing on my "why," I've realized compassion and adventure are really important to me. I think I have let those values fall to the wayside while I was focusing on pregnancy and my loss and everything else, but as I have been able to refocus on them, it has been so energizing.

_____

_____

_____

To move toward the life I want to create, I would like to take the following actions...

Example: Here are a few specific goals I would like to take: (1) I want to plan a trip to Mexico. I haven't traveled enough, and I need some adventure in my life. (2) I want to start volunteering at my local animal shelter. (3) I want to start working on self-compassion exercises. I have a self-compassion journal with prompts that I have not touched for years, so I want to start doing that daily. (4) I want to learn how to rollerblade!

_____

_____

_____

_____

What am I willing to endure to make this goal happen?

I am willing to endure these emotions…

Example: Anger, sadness, worry, anxiety, and frustration

_____

_____

_____

_____

I am willing to endure these thoughts…

Example: "I don't know if I have the energy to do this."
"What if people think I should be focusing on getting pregnant again?"
"What if I'm not good enough?"

_____

_____

_____

_____

I can count on the following allies and supports as I move toward these goals…

Example: I know if I announce these goals to my team at work, they will cheer me on and hold me gently accountable, so I will make a plan to do that. I also know my partner will be 100% supportive of this for me.

_____

_____

_____

_____

What are some barriers I can imagine getting in my way?

My internal barriers are…

Example: Me deciding that these goals aren't important enough and deciding that I need to focus on my job or others' needs before my own.

_____

_____

_____

_____

My external barriers are…

Example: My work can take up a lot of time, and there is always something to do. If I don't manage it or set boundaries, it could be a real barrier. I can also imagine some friends not understanding why I would choose these goals and questioning why I am not trying to have another baby immediately.

_____

_____

_____

_____

How do I want to manage some of these barriers? Steps I will take include…

Example: Reaching out to a friend (one of my supports and allies) if I need help. If I encounter a barrier, I will make sure I stop to pause, reflect, and write in my journal. That always helps me slow down and really figure out what I want.

_____

_____

_____

_____

What I would like to remind future me if I find myself struggling to reach these goals?

Example: I know it's hard, but remember you are doing the best you can. Anytime you question an action, ask yourself: Will this help me create the kind of life I want? You got this!

_____

_____

_____

_____

Let's Reach Our Goals!

Goal setting is not easy, and it can be incredibly beneficial to have the support of your family, friends, your therapist, or anyone else on your side who can build you up. It's also important to make goals as attainable as possible to create positive momentum for yourself. I have often seen individuals setting goals that are too big right off the bat, which leads to inevitable frustration and disappointment if they do not meet their established goals—and which then stops all forward progress. To increase your chances for success, consider the following tips as you begin working toward your goals:

- **Get an accountability buddy.** Ask your partner or another supportive person if they will help you reach this goal. For example, if your goal is to meditate more often, ask your accountability buddy if they would like to practice with you or if they are willing to check in with you at the end of the week to assess your progress.

- **Make your goals realistic and specific.** This is so vital! Define your goal by breaking it down into measurable components. For example, it's great if your goal is to eat healthy, but consider what you mean by this. Does this mean incorporating more fruits and vegetables into your diet, or does it mean limiting the number of times you eat out? Or does it mean both? Also, make those goals realistic! The idea of never eating out would be impossible for me and would just set me up for failure (Chick-fil-A® is a weekly occurrence in my family), but limiting take-out to two times a week is doable.

- **Shape your environment to the goals you are setting.** Want to start journaling? Put your journal somewhere accessible, such as on your nightstand, so it's easily available. Anything you can do to streamline meeting your goals will make them more likely to happen.

- **Find a system that works for you and stick to it.** There are tons of amazing supports out there when it comes to goal setting and planning, including apps like Habitica™, planners, reminders on your phone, and good old-fashioned to-do lists. Identify what system will be most helpful for you and make it happen!

Pregnancy After Loss

For many, the path after pregnancy loss may be to try becoming pregnant again. Regardless of how long we wait before we begin trying again, the process can be very anxiety provoking and scary. Additionally, women who have experienced previous pregnancy loss may be more likely to develop depression, anxiety, or posttraumatic stress in subsequent pregnancies (Gong et al., 2013). This makes sense seeing as pregnancy can already be emotionally challenging as we are confronted by completely new physical, emotional, logistical, and financial experiences. After miscarriage, this already stressful experience is compounded by fears around experiencing another loss.

After experiencing a miscarriage, we often fear having to go through another loss—to have to go through the emotional and physical trauma that lives alongside miscarriage. It is often this **anticipatory grief**—that is, the fear of or preparation for loss—that can be even more destructive for those who are pregnant after experiencing miscarriage. Indeed, many of my clients have told me that it was the anxiety and fears circulating through their mind about having another loss that was much more distressing to them than the actual experience of finding out that they were having another miscarriage.

Oftentimes, if I am helping clients navigate a challenging situation that they have been through before, I will encourage them to consider what mindset or actions they would like to repeat and what actions or attitudes need to stay in the past. For example, I will often ask this question when clients are starting to date after ending a relationship. They may note that they found it valuable to be with a partner who had similar religious values as them but did not find it helpful to date individuals who were often non-communicative from the beginning.

Similarly, I will ask clients who are pregnant after loss to consider what they want to bring with them from their previous pregnancy and what history they want to leave behind. For example, perhaps I want to repeat the decision to share the news of my pregnancy with my family and friends early on because it was helpful to have their support after my loss. Additionally, perhaps I want to leave behind my tendency to turn to the internet anytime I experience anxious thoughts and am hoping for some reassurance. Instead, I can write down all of my concerns and plan to ask my doctor about any specific questions I may have at my next appointment. While no two pregnancies will ever be the same, our history can be incredibly helpful in illuminating our path forward if we take the time to explore it.

A WALK TO REMEMBER

Take a walk down memory lane to write a letter to your past self. As a note, this exercise is intended for anyone hoping to gain self-compassion and clarity for their future, including those who are pregnant again after loss, those who are not pregnant, those who plan to become pregnant in the future, and those who are unsure of their path. When you consider your past self, allow feelings of compassion and kindness to flow through you. Remember it is likely that anything you did in the past made sense to you at the time. If you find yourself struggling to cultivate feelings of warmth and compassion, return to the self-compassion letter your wrote in Chapter 7, and read this letter to yourself a few more times until you find yourself able to receive compassion and acceptance.

For the letter in this exercise, I would like to you to consider what you would like to tell your past self. Include words of encouragement and hope, as well as specific actions that you would like your past self to take. Rather than just saying "Don't do xyz," offer an alternative, such as "When you feel anxious, instead of researching every symptom you may be experiencing, write down a list of all your concerns and give it to your partner to research so you don't go down that pesky rabbit hole." I have included an abbreviated version of my letter here to provide some guidance.

Dear Past Self,

Things really suck right now. I'm not going to sugarcoat anything because I know you have heard it all before. What I will do is give you some truths. The first is that you will get through this, though I know it doesn't feel like that today. When we contemplate the unimaginable, it feels like truly that: unimaginable to picture a world where we could be experiencing the kind of pain and loss we are experiencing now and keep on living. But you will and you do. Now, along the way, I know you have done things that gave you the briefest of comforts, some more helpful than others. No judgment here—you need what you need AND I know some of those things ended up kicking you in the butt later, so I want to offer a few suggestions.

First, when people offer you help, whether it be to bring you dinner or to take a task off of your hands, let them. I know it's not easy, and it is almost automatic to say, "No thanks, I got it," but this is a time where it's okay to not have it all together and to lean on those who care about you. Second, I know you often try to stop yourself anytime you have felt even the tiniest twinge of pain, and you think that being hopeful is going to cause more pain for you in the end. I am here to tell you that is unfortunately nonsense. Being hopeful provided you with some much needed light in an otherwise pretty dark place, so allow yourself to be hopeful knowing the pain will be there no matter what, and it's that hope that gives you some cushion when you feel like you are falling.

I know I said no sugarcoating, and I'm going to hold to that. I do want to encourage you to feel everything you are feeling and to know that it is 100% okay to not show up as your "normal" self right now. Take rest and take care knowing that things will suck for a while, and then be kind of okay, and then probably suck again. Through all of that, YOU WILL BE OKAY. Just in case you needed to hear that reminder.

Now take some time to write your past self a letter in the space here:

Dear Past Self,

_____

_____

_____

_____

_____

_____

_____

_____

_____

_____

_____

_____

_____

_____

_____

_____

_____

_____

_____

_____

_____

_____

Based on these reflections, what changes or directions would you like to make?

_____

_____

_____

_____

Looking to the Future

Now I want you to write a letter to your future self. Consider what your future self will be doing, feeling, and looking forward to. Imagine all of the specific joys and obstacles that will be coming your way. I have included my letter as an example.

Dear Future Self,

Yes, you are reading that correctly. There is no letter written to my future self because the future has not happened yet. We still get to make it what we wish it to be. We still have the power to move toward our dreams and our goals, even as we endure challenges and pain along the way. I mentioned this previously, and I will say it again because it is that important: I am not asking you to be optimistic about your past. What happened was painful and horrible, and nothing will diminish your loss. *What I am asking you now is to be optimistic about your future. Be optimistic about your strengths, your supports, and your dreams that got you to this point.* Recognize that the very fact that you are reading this and have gone through this workbook shows your willingness, compassion, and courage to confront your losses and pain and to become an active agent of whatever comes next. I know it will be amazing.

Notes for Therapists

The process of grieving takes time, and there is no prescribed way to move through the stages of grief. Many clients, particularly those who tend to over-function in the face of distress, may want to move quickly toward meaning making as a way to avoid experiencing the pain of their loss. Be sure to use clinical judgment and insight to help clients identify and understand where they are at in the grieving process, and match the interventions you offer to that level.

For instance, you may be helping a client identify their next steps forward, but in doing so, you notice the client continuing to perseverate around the loss and how devastating it feels that their original dreams have been deterred. According to grief expert David Kessler (2019), we become stuck in grief when we don't feel witnessed. That means that if you have a client who is struggling to determine their next steps forward, it may be an indication that their grief has not been fully witnessed, either internally or externally. For example, perhaps they are craving the witnessing of their partner or loved one, or perhaps they have received support from their loved ones but have not allowed for an internal witnessing of their grief.

Essentially, take a moment to consider how any resistance you may be experiencing from the client is related to where they are at in the grieving process, as well as any number of other relevant clinical factors, such as their sense of safety and connection in the therapeutic relationship.

Additionally, make sure that clients feel empowered to be as creative as possible when considering their "how." As I mentioned at the beginning of this book, we become an active participant in our grief when we start imagining different paths we can take in our stories. Allow your clients to imagine paths they may have never considered before. It does not mean that they will ultimately take those paths, but it is incredibly important for clients to have the space and freedom to consider all their options.

REFERENCES

For your convenience, the worksheets and forms from this book are available for download at www.pesi.com/miscarriagemapworkbook

Boerner, K., Mancini, A. D., & Bonanno, G. A. (2013). On the nature and prevalence of uncomplicated and complicated patterns of grief. In M. Stroebe, H. Schut, & J. van den Bout (Eds.), *Complicated grief: Scientific foundations for health care professionals* (pp. 55–68). New York: Routledge.

Bowins, B. E. (2012). Therapeutic dissociation: Compartmentalization and absorption. *Counselling Psychology Quarterly, 25*(3), 307–317.

Bowlby, J. (1969). *Attachment and loss: Attachment* (Vol. 1). New York: Basic Books.

Brown, B. (2008). *I thought it was just me (but it isn't): Making the journey from "What will people think?" to "I am enough."* New York: Avery.

Brown, B. (2018). *Dare to lead: Brave work. Tough conversations. Whole hearts.* New York: Random House.

Burgard, D. (2011). *Finding your inner parent: A meditation.* Retrieved from www.bodypositive.com/meditation_p.htm

Devine, M. (2017). *It's OK that you're not OK: Meeting grief and loss in a culture that doesn't understand.* Boulder, CO: Sounds True Publishing.

Doka, K. J. (1989). *Disenfranchised grief: Recognizing hidden sorrow.* Lexington, MA: Lexington Press.

Engel, B. (2014, July 13). How compassion can heal shame from childhood. *Psychology Today.* Retrieved from https://www.psychologytoday.com/us/blog/the-compassion-chronicles/201307/how-compassion-can-heal-shame-childhood

Gong, X., Hao, J., Tao, F., Zhang, J., Wang, H., & Xu, R. (2013). Pregnancy loss and anxiety and depression during subsequent pregnancies: Data from the C-ABC study. *European Journal of Obstetrics & Gynecology and Reproductive Biology, 166*(1), 30–36.

Gottman, J. M., & Gottman, J. S. (2008). Gottman method couple therapy. In A. S. Gurman (Ed.), *Clinical handbook of couple therapy* (pp. 138–164). New York: Guilford Press.

Harris, R. (2013). *The complete set of client handouts and worksheets from ACT books.* Retrieved from https://thehappinesstrap.com/upimages/Complete_Worksheets_2014.pdf

Hayes, S. C., Strosahl, K. D., & Wilson, K. G. (2009). *Acceptance and commitment therapy.* Washington, DC: American Psychological Association.

Hayes, S. C., Wilson, K. G., Gifford, E. V., Follette, V. M., & Strosahl, K. (1996). Experiential avoidance and behavioral disorders: A functional dimensional approach to diagnosis and treatment. *Journal of Consulting and Clinical Psychology, 64*(6), 1152–1168.

Jaffe, J., Diamond, M. O., & Diamond, D. J. (2005). *Unsung lullabies: Understanding and coping with infertility.* New York: St. Martin's Press.

James, J., & Friedman, R., (2017). *The grief recovery handbook: The action program for moving beyond death, divorce, and other losses including health, career, and faith.* New York: HarperCollins.

Jankowski, K. F., & Takahashi, H. (2014). Cognitive neuroscience of social emotions and implications for psychopathology: Examining embarrassment, guilt, envy, and schadenfreude. *Psychiatry and Clinical Neurosciences, 68*(5), 319–336.

Kessler, D. (2019). *Finding meaning: The sixth stage of grief.* New York: Scribner.

Kübler-Ross, E., & Kessler, D. (2005). *On grief and grieving: Finding the meaning of grief through the five stages of loss.* New York: Simon and Schuster.

Maslow, A. H. (1943). A theory of human motivation. *Psychological Review, 50*(4), 370–396.

Neff, K. D. (2009). Self-compassion. In M. R. Leary & R. H. Hoyle (Eds.), *Handbook of individual differences in social behavior* (pp. 561–573). New York: Guilford Press.

Neff, K. D. (2011). Self-compassion, self-esteem, and well-being. *Social and Personality Psychology Compass, 5*(1), 1–12.

Resick, P. A., & Schnicke, M. K. (1992). Cognitive processing therapy for sexual assault victims. *Journal of Consulting and Clinical Psychology, 60*(5), 748–756.

Rogers, C. (1961). *On becoming a person: A therapist's view of psychotherapy*. Boston: Houghton Mifflin Company.

Schlessinger, L. (2019, December 5). *Self-soothing vs. self-care—Is there a difference?* Retrieved from www.well.org/mindset/self-soothing-vs-self-care-is-there-a-difference/

Shreffler, K. M., Hill, P. W., & Cacciatore, J. (2012). Explaining increased odds of divorce following miscarriage or stillbirth. *Journal of Divorce and Remarriage, 53*, 91–107.

Swanson, K. M., Karmali, Z. A., Powell, S. H., & Pulvermakher, F. (2003). Miscarriage effects on couples' interpersonal and sexual relationships during the first year after loss: Women's perceptions. *Psychosomatic Medicine, 65*(5), 902–910.

Wojnar, D. M., Swanson, K. M., & Adolfsson, A. S. (2011). Confronting the inevitable: A conceptual model of miscarriage for use in clinical practice and research. *Death Studies, 35*(6), 536–558.

Made in the USA
Las Vegas, NV
02 October 2024

96105279R00090